Playground Equipment

DATE

PLAYGROUND EQUIPMENT

Do-It-Yourself, Indestructible, Practically Free

Written and Designed by
Lloyd Marston

Illustrations and Layout by
Gerlinder Henn

Jefferson, N.C., and London
McFarland & Company, Inc., Publishers

Library of Congress Cataloging in Publication Data

Marston, Lloyd.
  Playground equipment.

  1. Playgrounds—Equipment and supplies. 2. Play-
grounds—Design and construction. I. Title. II. Henn,
Gerlinder, illus.
GV426.5.M37 1984   688.7′6′068   83-25565

ISBN 0-89950-104-4

Manufactured in the United States of America

McFarland & Company, Inc., Publishers
  Box 611, Jefferson, North Carolina 28640

46519

Table of Contents

Introduction

A good playground literally becomes "all things to all children." There are certain characteristics shared by all well designed play areas. These characteristics are felt immediately by children who enter the area.

The first impression is spontaneity of play. The child must be attracted to the area and drawn into its activities. Play must be spontaneous because play must be voluntary; it cannot be forced. Play is nature's way of teaching the child how to use its body. The playground shows the child how play interacts with the environment. The playground teaches the child to progress from "doing his own thing" to interaction and "associative play." It is at this level that we can observe "dramatic play" in which the players define who they are through experimental role-playing. It is during this process that they can learn and develop behavior for the social consequences of their actions. In the setting of definite space and a secure environment (the playground), children are free to pursue their natural role-playing, which leads them to social reality.

The most stimulating kind of play is active, involving real physical risks. It develops physical competence and endurance. Traditional playground areas activate this physical play and concentrate its essence in a creative way to provide for the social growth needs of the children.

There are hundreds of other words used to describe movements. Obviously play or movement must be one of the more important activities of man. Consequently we should take some time to develop activities. Common sense and a little forethought are all that are needed to use this book correctly.

First. Determine the age group of the children and pick your equipment accordingly.

Second. Allow 25 sq. ft. per child for play area. If play is closely supervised and structural, then less area can be used.

BLINK	CLUTCH	SNATCH	WIGGLE	CHEW
SLAP	WRIGGLE	FROWN	THROW	KICK
GRIN	FLING	SHUFFLE	SQUIRM	GAPE
STAMP	STRETCH	GLARE	BEAT	TRAMPLE
GRIMACE	WHIP	TIP-TOE	TWIST	LEER
SCUFF	TURN	POUT	WAVE	SLIP
SCOWL	PUNCH	MINCE	DROP	YAWN
LIFT	STUMBLE	COLLAPSE	WINCE	REACH
TAP	FALL	SQUIRT	GROPE	DRAG
SHAKE	WINK	WEAVE	DANCE	SWING
POUND	OPEN	PAT	SWAY	STRIDE
CLAPS	PINCH	BOUNCE	GRIND	CLENCH
POINT	BOB	SWEEP	GRAB	POKE
CREEP	OUT	STROKE	PLUCK	CRAWL
SLICE	SCRATCH	BECKON	WALK	CHOP
SQUEEZE	CLOSE	RUN	PUSH	WRING
PICK	SKIP	THRUST	KNEAD	RUB

Third. Choose an appropriate site. It should be well drained, safe, easily accessible, secure from traffic, easily seen, etc.

Fourth. Group your equipment so that the children have a variety of activities, i.e. sliding, swinging, climbing, hanging, crawling, etc.

Fifth. Many of the materials shown in this book are free. Be choosey. Take your time and pick the best materials. Remember, the child's safety depends on your choice of materials.

Sixth. Anyone can build a playground. The actual process is just as important to you as the finished product is to the child.

Seventh. Provide as wide a range of different equipment as possible. All it takes is a little imagination.

Remember that play is a child's work

Material Specifications

Wood

All timbers should be No. 2 grade southern pine or equivalent unless otherwise specified and should be treated with CCA according to the American Wood Preservers Association standards for LP-22 (in ground use).

Round timbers should be southern pine, treated with penta-cholorophenal, and have diameters measuring from four to eight inches.

Hardware

All hardware, bolts, nuts, washers, pipes, and fittings should be galvanized or zinc-plated. Firemen's poles should be made from two-inch diameter galvanized pipe, with ends capped, and should be embedded two feet in concrete. Overhead climbs should be made from one-inch galvanized pipe with ends hidden and secured.

Slides

Slides should be manufactured from 26 gauge (minimum) stainless or galvanized metal, constructed with all metal edges hidden; two-by-ten railings give adequate protection.

Tires

Tires should have drainage holes and contain no steel belts.

Method of Construction

All uprights are sunk to a depth of two feet in concrete, unless otherwise specified. Edges to be rounded with a ⅜" radius and exposed ends are chamfered. All timbers are joined with lag bolts or bolts and nuts, with exposed bolts and nuts countersunk flush with surface of wood. Ends of bolts are to be peened to prevent removal and lock nuts should be used where advisable. Galvanized nails are to be used for nailed constructions.

Children's Size Graph

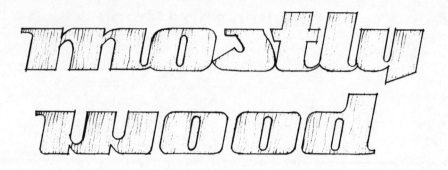

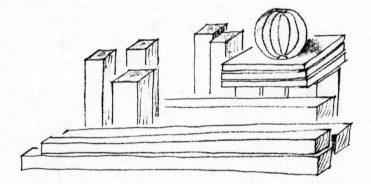

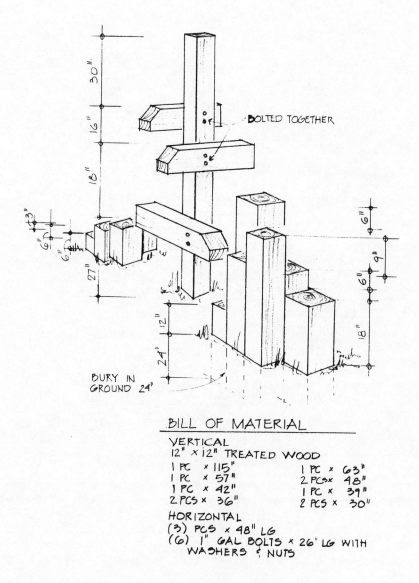

BOLTED TOGETHER

BURY IN
GROUND 24"

BILL OF MATERIAL

VERTICAL
12" × 12" TREATED WOOD

1 PC × 115"	1 PC × 63"
1 PC × 57"	2 PCS × 48"
1 PC × 42"	1 PC × 39"
2 PCS × 36"	2 PCS × 30"

HORIZONTAL
(3) PCS × 48" LG
(6) 1" GAL BOLTS × 26" LG WITH
    WASHERS & NUTS

LOG WALK

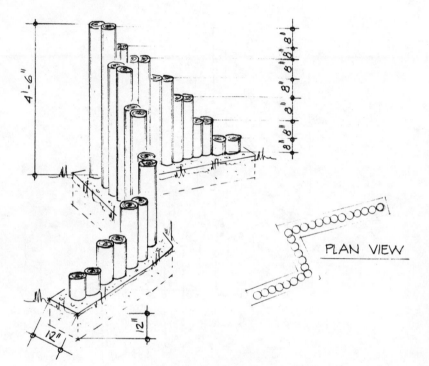

PLAN VIEW

BILL OF MATERIAL

(20) 90# BAGS OF READY MIX CEMENT
(4) 8" φ TREATED WOOD POLES × 16" LG
(4) 8" φ   "   "   "   × 24" "
(4) 8" φ   "   "   "   × 32" LG
(4) 8" φ   "   "   "   × 40" "
(4) 8" φ   "   "   "   × 48" LG
(4) 8" φ   "   "   "   × 56" "
(2) 8" φ   "   "   "   × 64" LG

8

BENCH

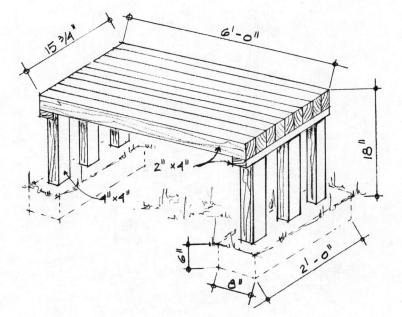

15 3/4"
6'-0"
18"
2" × 4"
4" × 4"
6"
8"
2'-0"

BILL OF MATERIAL

(4) 90# BAGS OF CEMENT
(9) PCS OF 2×4 TREATED WOOD × 72" LG
(6) PCS OF 4×4   "   " ×12" LG
(2) PCS OF 2×4   "   ' ×15 3/4" LG
GAL NAILS TO SUIT

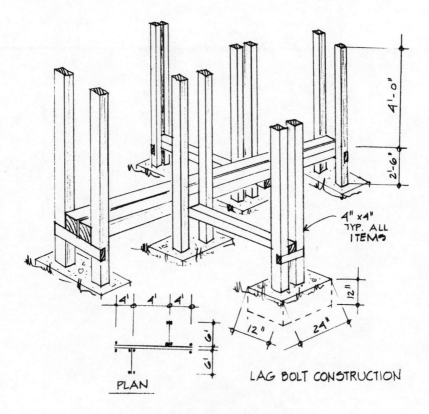

PLAN

LAG BOLT CONSTRUCTION

4" x4"
TYP. ALL
ITEMS

BILL OF MATERIAL

(12) 4" x4" TREATED WOOD POSTS x 80"
(2) 4" x4"   "   "   x 72"
(2) 4" x4"   "   "   x 144"
(2) 4" x4"   "   "   x 16"
(4) 4" x4"   "   "   x 12"
(40) 1/2" LAG BOLTS (ZINC PLATED) x 7" LG
(12) 90# BAGS OF CEMENT

HANGING BRIDGE

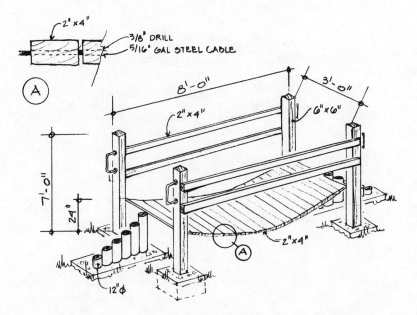

2" x 4"

3/8" DRILL
5/16" GAL STEEL CABLE

A

8'-0"

3'-0"

2" x 4"

6" x 6"

7'-0"

24"

12" φ

A

2" x 4"

BILL OF MATERIAL

(10) 90# BAGS OF CEMENT
(4) 6" x 6" TREATED WOOD x 8'-0"
(4) 2" x 4"   "   "   x 8'-0"
(24) 2" x 4" x 40" LG TREATED WOOD
(4) 5/8" EYE BOLT x 8" LG.
(2) 5/16" GAL STEEL CABLE x 10'-0"
(2) 12" φ TREATED WOOD POLE x 8"
(2) 12" φ   "   "   "   x 12"
(2) 12" φ   "   "   "   x 16"
(2) 12" φ   "   "   "   x 20"
(2) 12" φ   "   "   "   x 24"
(2) 12" φ   "   "   "   x 28"

EARLY SLIDE

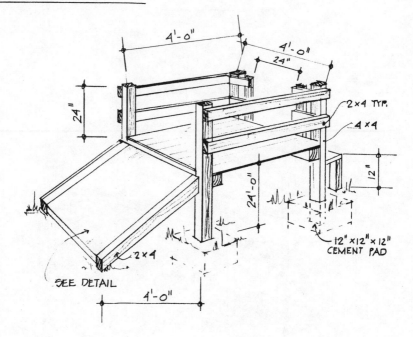

4'-0"

4'-0"

24"

24"

2×4 TYP.

4×4

24'-0"

12"

2×4

SEE DETAIL

12"×12"×12"
CEMENT PAD

4'-0"

BILL OF MATERIAL

NAIL TO SUIT
(8) 90# BAGS OF CEMENT
SLIDE
(2) 2×4 TREATED WOOD × 48" LG
(8) 3/8 ×1" LAG BOLTS
(1) 1/8 THK AL × 40 1/2" WD × 52"LG
   WELDED AS SHOWN
LEGS
(4) 4×4 TREATED WOOD × 60"LG
OTHER
(18) 2×4 TREATED WOOD × 48" LG
(4)   "   "   "   × 12" LG
(2)   "   "   "   × 24" LG

EARLY SLIDE
- DETAILS -

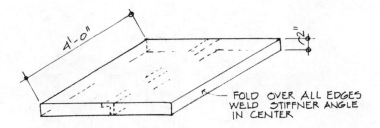

4'-0"

2"

FOLD OVER ALL EDGES
WELD STIFFNER ANGLE
IN CENTER

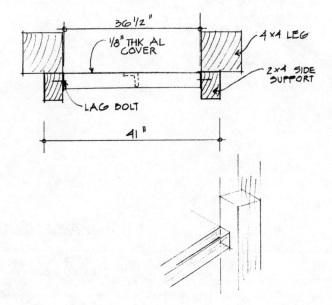

36½"

⅛" THK AL COVER

4×4 LEG

2×4 SIDE SUPPORT

LAG BOLT

41"

SEE-SAW GIRAFFE

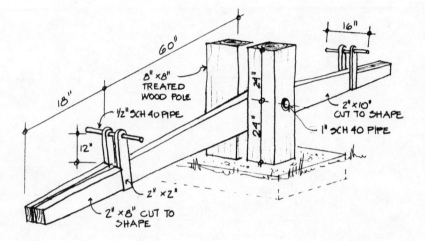

18"

60"

8"×8"
TREATED
WOOD POLE

½" SCH 40 PIPE

12"

2"×2"

2"×8" CUT TO
SHAPE

24" 24"

24"

16"

2"×10"
CUT TO SHAPE

1" SCH 40 PIPE

BILL OF MATERIAL

(2) 8"×8"×6'-0" TREATED WOOD POLES
(1) 2"×10" TREATED WOOD × 13'-6"
(4) 2"×8"   "   " × 18"
(4) 2"×2"   "   " × 18"
 2 ½"⌀ SCH 40 PIPE × 16"
 1 1"⌀ SCH 40 PIPE × 22"

TREE HOUSE

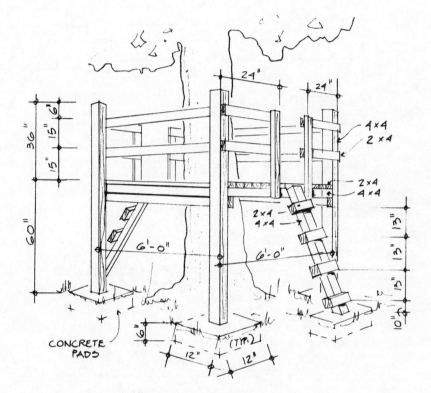

BILL OF MATERIAL

PLATFORM
(4) PCS 4"x4" TREATED WOOD x 102" LG
(2)   "   "   "   "   "   x 72" LG
(2)   "   "   "   "   "   x 64" LG
(16) PCS 2x4"   "   "   x 72" LG
LADDERS
(2) PCS 4"x4" TREATED WOOD x 66" LG
(8)   "   2"x4"   "   "   x 24" LG
HANDRAIL
(8) PCS 2"x4" TREATED WOOD x 24" LG
(4) "   2"x4"   "   "   x 34" LG
(4) "   2"x4"   "   "   x 72" LG
(8) 90# BAGS OF READY MIX CEMENT
GAL NAILS TO SUIT

LOOK-OUT TOWER

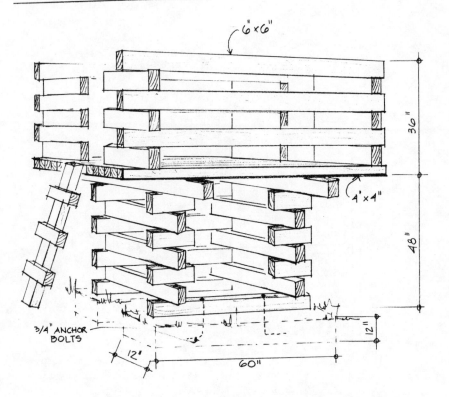

6"×6"

36"

4"×4"

48"

3/4" ANCHOR BOLTS

12"

12"

60"

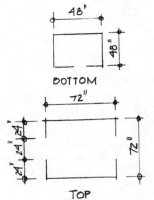

48"

48"

BOTTOM

72"

24" 24" 24"

72"

TOP

BILL OF MATERIAL

(10) 90# BAGS OF READY MIX CEMENT
(4) 3/4" ANCHOR BOLTS × 18" LG WITH
     FLAT WASHERS & NUTS
BOTTOM SECTION
(11) PCS 6"×6" TREATED WOOD × 48"
(6) PCS   "   "   " × 12'
(2) PCS   "   "   " × 72"
TOP SECTION
(6) PCS 6"×6" TREATED WOOD × 72"
(12) PCS   "   "   " × 24"
(16) PCS 4"×4"   "   ' × 72"
NAILS OR LAG BOLTS TO SUIT

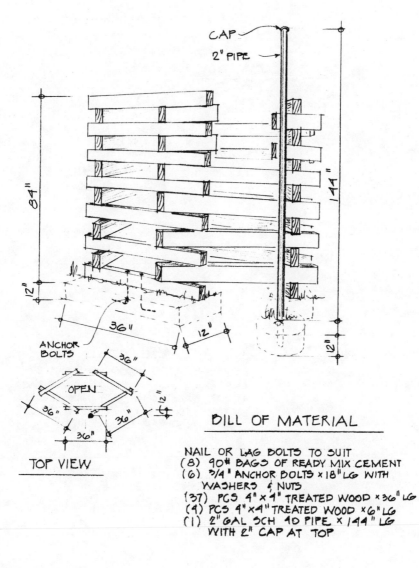

CAP

2" PIPE

84"

144"

12"

36"

12"

12"

ANCHOR BOLTS

36"

OPEN

36"

36"

36"

12"

TOP VIEW

BILL OF MATERIAL

NAIL OR LAG BOLTS TO SUIT
(8) 90# BAGS OF READY MIX CEMENT
(6) 3/4" ANCHOR BOLTS x 18" LG WITH
    WASHERS & NUTS
(37) PCS 4" x 4" TREATED WOOD x 36" LG
(4) PCS 4" x 4" TREATED WOOD x 6" LG
(1) 2" GAL SCH 40 PIPE x 144" LG
    WITH 2" CAP AT TOP

VAULTING BAR

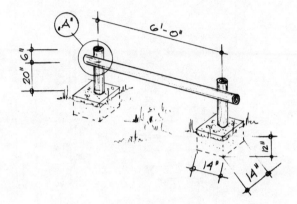

BILL OF MATERIAL

(2) 8" ⌀ TREATED WOOD POLES × 38"
(1) 8" ⌀   "   "   POLE × 7'-0"
(4) 90# BAGS OF READY MIX CEMENT
(2) 1" BOLTS GAL × 16" LONG WITH (2)
     FLAT WASHERS & (1) HEX NUT

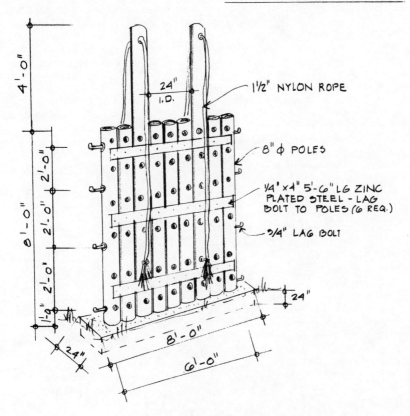

1½" NYLON ROPE

24" I.D.

8" φ POLES

¼" × 4" 5'-6" LG ZINC PLATED STEEL - LAG BOLT TO POLES (6 REQ.)

¾" LAG BOLT

4'-0"

2'-0"

2'-0"

6'-0"

2'-0"

2'-0"

1'-0"

24"

24"

8'-0"

6'-0"

BILL OF MATERIAL

(2) 8" φ TREATED WOOD POLES × 14'
(7) 8" φ " " " × 10'
(2) 1½" φ NYLON ROPE × 20' LG
(8) ¾" LAG BOLTS × 18" LG
(6) ¼" × 4" × 66" LG - ZINC PLATED STEEL
(54) ½ × 3" LAG BOLT ZINC PLATED
(8) 90# BAG OF READY MIX CEMENT

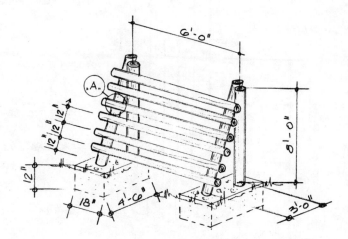

BILL OF MATERIAL

(2) 8" ⌀ TREATED WOOD POLE × 9'-0" LG
(2) 8" ⌀   "   "   " × 9'-6"   "
(6) 8" ⌀   "   ·   " × 7'-0"   "
(20) 90# BAGS OF READY MIX CEMENT
(16) 1" BOLTS GAL × 16" LG WITH (2) FLAT
     WASHERS & (1) HEX NUT

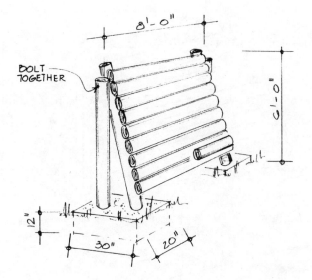

BILL OF MATERIAL

(2) 6" ⌀ TREATED WOOD POLES × 7'-0"
(2) 6" ⌀   "   "   " × 8'-0"
(9) 6" ⌀   "   "   " × 9'-0"
(1) 6" ⌀   "   "   " × 4'-0"
(22) 3/4 PLATED BOLTS ×15" LG WITH
FLAT WASHERS & NUTS
(6) 90# BAGS OF READY MIX CEMENT

DOUBLE CLIMB WALL

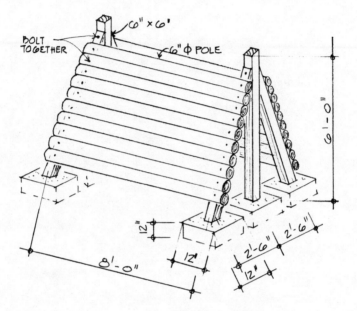

BILL OF MATERIAL

(6) 90# BAGS OF READY MIX CEMENT
(2) 6" x 6" TREATED WOOD x 8'-0"
(4) 6" x 6"   "   "   x 9'-0"
(20) 6" ø   "   POLES x 9'-0"
(44) 3/4" PLATED BOLT x 15" LG WITH
     FLAT WASHERS & NUTS

BEAM TRAVERSE

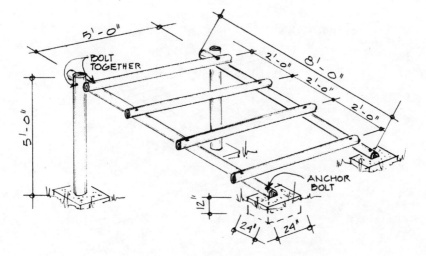

BILL OF MATERIAL

(2) 3/4" × 18" LG ANCHOR BOLTS
(10) 3/4" PLATED BOLTS × 14" COMPLETE
    WITH FLAT WASHERS & NUTS
(6) 90# BAGS OF READY MIX CEMENT
(6) 6"⌀ TREATED WOOD POLES × 6'-0"
(2) 6"⌀   "   "   " × 9'-0"

BALANCE BEAM

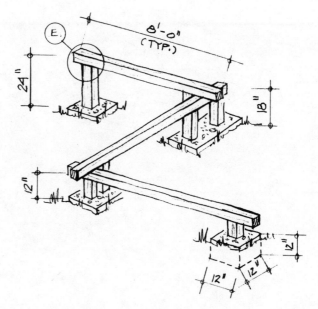

BILL OF MATERIAL

(3) 4" x 4" TREATED WOOD BEAM x 8'-0" LG.
(2)   "   "   "   "   x 30" LG
(2)   "   "   "   "   x 24" LG
(2)   "   "   "   "   x 18" LG
(16) 1/2" LAG BOLT x 8" LG - GALVANIZED
(8) 90# BAGS OF CEMENT

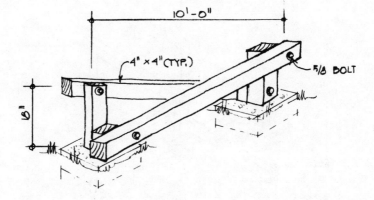

10'-0"

4" × 4" (TYP.)

5/8 BOLT

18"

BILL OF MATERIAL

(2) 4"×4" TREATED WOOD POLES ×10'-6"
(2) 4"×4"   "   "   "   × 30"
(2) 4"×4"   "   "   "   × 18"
(2) 5/8 HEX BOLTS × 14" LG
(2) 5/8 "   "   × 10" LG
(4) 90# BAGS OF CEMENT

25

FOUR-WAY BEAM

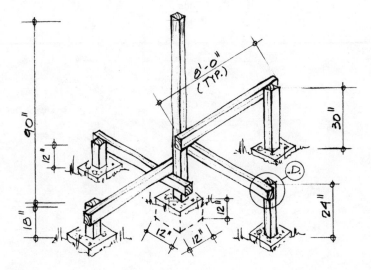

BILL OF MATERIAL

(10) 90# BAGS OF CEMENT
(8) 3/4" GAL BOLTS × 9" LG W/ FLAT WASHERS AND NUTS
(4) 4" × 4" TREATED WOOD BEAMS × 8'-0" LG.
(1) " " " " × 8'-6" LG
(1) " " " " × 18"
(1) " " " " × 24"
(1) " " " " × 30"
(1) " " " " × 36"

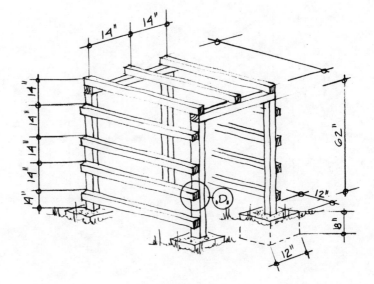

BILL OF MATERIAL

(11) PCS 4"×4" TREATED WOOD × 5'-0"
(2) PCS 4"×4"   "   "   × 2'-4"
(4) PCS 4"×4"   "   "   × 6'-2"
(22) 3/4" GAL BOLTS ×9" LG W/FLAT
     WASHERS AND HEX NUTS
(8) 90# BAGS OF CEMENT

LOG PILE

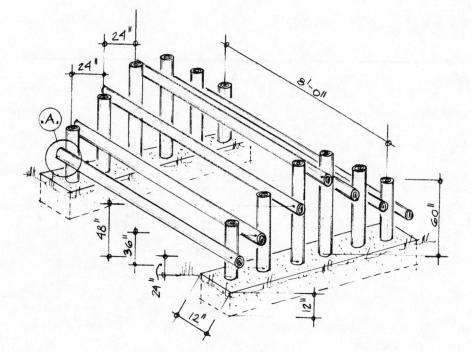

BILL OF MATERIAL

(7) 8" ⌀ TREATED WOOD POLES × 10'-0" LG
(4) 8" ⌀ " " " × 42" "
(4) 8" ⌀ " " " × 60" "
(4) 8" ⌀ " " " × 96" "
(20) 90# BAGS OF READY MIX CEMENT
(14) 1" BOLTS GAL × 16" LG WITH (2) FLAT
     WASHERS & (1) HEX NUT

LOG JUMP

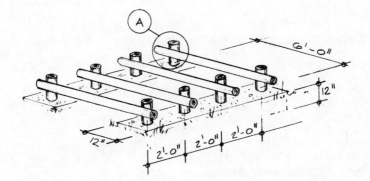

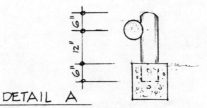

DETAIL A

BILL OF MATERIAL

(8) 8"⌀ TREATED WOOD POLE
    2'-0" LG
(4) 8"⌀ TREATED WOOD POLE
    7'-0" LG
(8) 1" BOLTS GAL × 16" LONG WITH
    2 FLAT WASHERS & (1) HEX NUT
(20) 90# BAGS OF READY MIX
              CEMENT

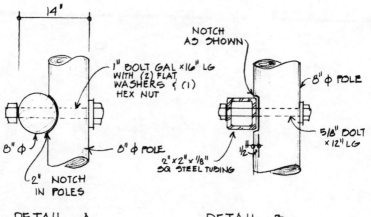

14"

1" BOLT GAL ×16" LG
WITH (2) FLAT
WASHERS & (1)
HEX NUT

NOTCH
AS SHOWN

8" φ POLE

5/8" BOLT
×12" LG

8" φ

8" φ POLE

2" NOTCH
IN POLES

2"×2"×1/8"
SQ STEEL TUBING

1/2"

DETAIL .A.

DETAIL .B.

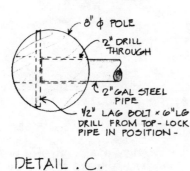

8" φ POLE

2" DRILL
THROUGH

2" GAL STEEL
PIPE

1/2" LAG BOLT × 6" LG
DRILL FROM TOP- LOCK
PIPE IN POSITION -

DETAIL . C.

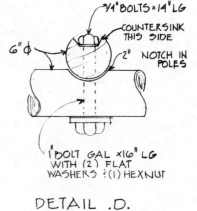

3/4" BOLTS ×14" LG

COUNTERSINK
THIS SIDE

6" φ

2" NOTCH IN
POLES

1" BOLT GAL ×16" LG
WITH (2) FLAT
WASHERS & (1) HEXNUT

DETAIL .D.

30

LOG CONSTRUCTION
DETAILS

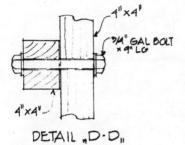

4"×4"

¾" GAL BOLT
× 9" LG

4"×4"

DETAIL „D·D„

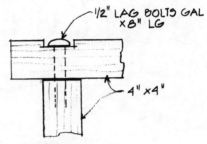

½" LAG BOLTS GAL
×8" LG

4"×4"

DETAIL „E„

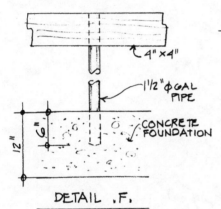

4"×4"

1½" ∅ GAL PIPE

CONCRETE FOUNDATION

6"

12"

DETAIL „F„

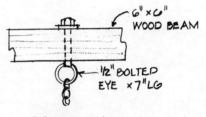

6"×6"
WOOD BEAM

½" BOLTED
EYE ×7"LG

DETAIL „H„

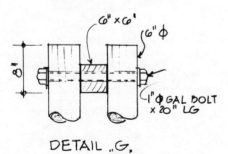

6"×6"

6"∅

8"

1"∅ GAL BOLT
× 20" LG

DETAIL „G„

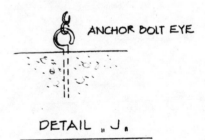

ANCHOR BOLT EYE

DETAIL „J„

tire stacking

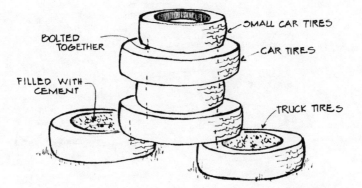

SMALL CAR TIRES

CAR TIRES

BOLTED
TOGETHER

FILLED WITH
CEMENT

TRUCK TIRES

BILL OF MATERIAL
(4) 90# BAGS OF CEMENT
2 TRUCK TIRES
2 LARGE CAR TIRES
2 SMALL CAR TIRES
20 1/2" HEX HEAD MACHINE
BOLTS x 2" LONG

TIRE STACK 2

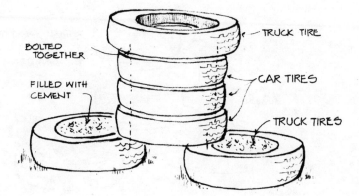

BOLTED
TOGETHER

FILLED WITH
CEMENT

TRUCK TIRE

CAR TIRES

TRUCK TIRES

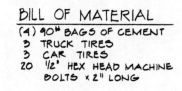

BILL OF MATERIAL
(4) 90ᴺ BAGS OF CEMENT
3 TRUCK TIRES
3 CAR TIRES
20 1/2" HEX HEAD MACHINE
    BOLTS x 2" LONG

TIRE STACK 3

TRUCK TIRE

CAR TIRES

TRUCK TIRES

CAR TIRES

BOLTED
TOGETHER

FILLED WITH
CEMENT

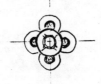

TOP VIEW OF
BOTTOM LAYER

ALTERNATIVE

TOP VIEW OF
SECOND ROW

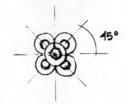

45°

BILL OF MATERIAL

(8) 90# BAGS OF CEMENT
8 CAR TIRES
3 TRUCK TIRES
24 1/2" HEX HEAD MACHINE
BOLTS × 2" LONG

TIRE STACK 4

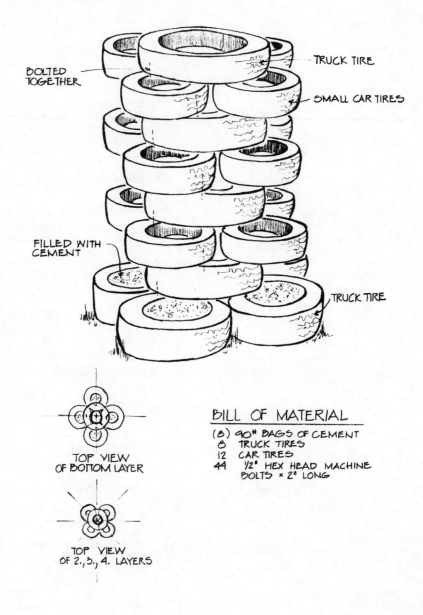

BOLTED
TOGETHER

TRUCK TIRE

SMALL CAR TIRES

FILLED WITH
CEMENT

TRUCK TIRE

TOP VIEW
OF BOTTOM LAYER

TOP VIEW
OF 2., 3., 4. LAYERS

BILL OF MATERIAL

(8) 90# BAGS OF CEMENT
8   TRUCK TIRES
12 CAR TIRES
44 ½" HEX HEAD MACHINE
    BOLTS × 2" LONG

TIRE STACK 5

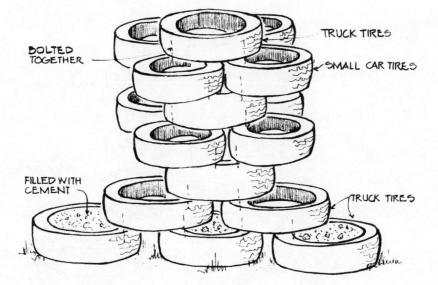

BOLTED
TOGETHER

TRUCK TIRES

SMALL CAR TIRES

FILLED WITH
CEMENT

TRUCK TIRES

TOP VIEW OF
BOTTOM LAYER

BILL OF MATERIAL

(6) 90# BAGS OF CEMENT
8 TRUCK TIRES
8 CAR TIRES
36 1/2" HEX HEAD MACHINE
BOLTS × 2" LONG

TOP VIEW OF
STACK LAYERS

TIRE STACK 6

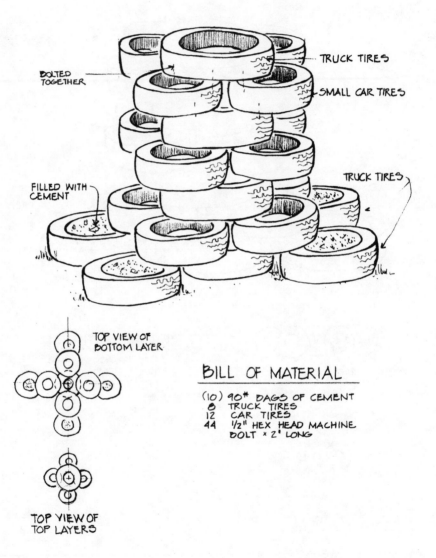

TRUCK TIRES

SMALL CAR TIRES

BOLTED TOGETHER

TRUCK TIRES

FILLED WITH CEMENT

TOP VIEW OF BOTTOM LAYER

TOP VIEW OF TOP LAYERS

BILL OF MATERIAL

(10) 90# BAGS OF CEMENT
8 TRUCK TIRES
12 CAR TIRES
44 1/2" HEX HEAD MACHINE BOLT × 2" LONG

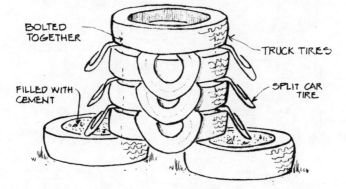

BOLTED TOGETHER

TRUCK TIRES

FILLED WITH CEMENT

SPLIT CAR TIRE

SPLIT TOP AND BOTTOM
OF TIRE WITH SHARP
KNIFE
END RESULT WILL
BE A FLAT DISC

BILL OF MATERIAL

(4) 90# BAGS OF CEMENT
6 TRUCK TIRES
12 SPLITS OF CAR TIRES
16 1/2" HEX HEAD MACHINE
BOLTS x 2" LONG

TIRE STACK 8

BOLTED TOGETHER

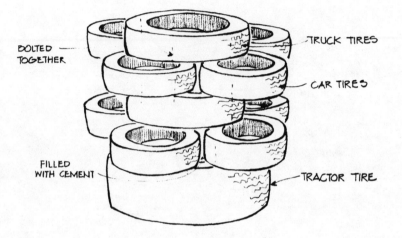

TRUCK TIRES

CAR TIRES

FILLED WITH CEMENT

TRACTOR TIRE

TOP VIEW

BILL OF MATERIAL

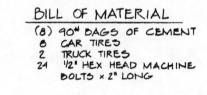

(8) 90# BAGS OF CEMENT
8   CAR TIRES
2   TRUCK TIRES
24   1/2" HEX HEAD MACHINE
     BOLTS x 2" LONG

40

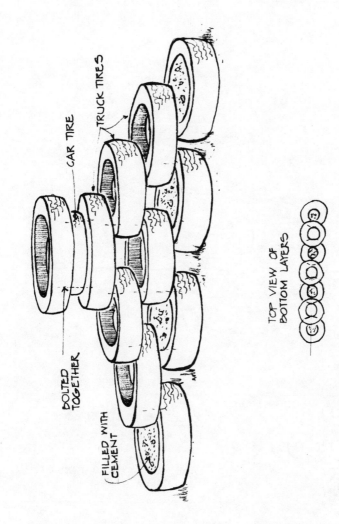

TRUCK TIRES

CAR TIRE

BOLTED TOGETHER

FILLED WITH CEMENT

TOP VIEW OF BOTTOM LAYERS

TOP VIEW OF TOP LAYERS

BILL OF MATERIAL

(8) 90# BAGS OF CEMENT
11 TRUCK TIRES
1   CAR TIRE
36 1/2" HEX HEAD MACHINE
    BOLTS × 2" LONG

TIRE STACK 10

BOLTED TOGETHER

CAR TIRE

TRUCK TIRES

FILLED WITH CEMENT

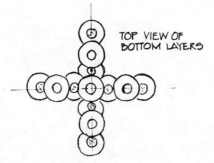

TOP VIEW OF BOTTOM LAYERS

BILL OF MATERIAL

(16) 90# BAGS OF CEMENT
18   TRUCK TIRES
1   CAR TIRE
48   1/2" HEX HEAD MACHINE
     BOLTS x 2" LONG

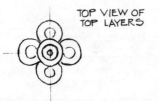

TOP VIEW OF TOP LAYERS

TUNNEL CRAWL-THROUGH

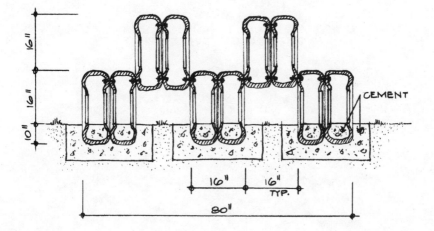

16"

16"

10"

CEMENT

16"

16"

TYP.

80"

BILL OF MATERIAL

(4) 90# BAGS OF CEMENT

(28) 3/8 × 3" HEX. H.D. BOLTS, NUTS, FLAT WASHERS

(10) TIRES

ESTIMATED LABOR
(1 MAN) 8 HRS

TYPICAL TIRE-TO-TIRE BOLTED CONNECTION

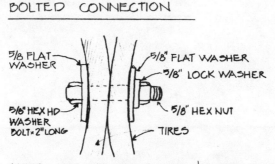

5/8 FLAT WASHER

5/8" FLAT WASHER

5/8" LOCK WASHER

5/8" HEX HD WASHER BOLT × 2" LONG

5/8" HEX NUT

TIRES

NOTE: ALL WASHERS, NUTS & BOLTS TO BE STD STEEL, ZINC PLATED

TYPICAL TIRE NOTE

1. IF TIRE IS IN VERTICAL POSITION SLOTS MUST BE PLACED IN BOTTOM FOR DRAINAGE

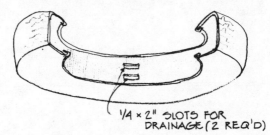

1/4 × 2" SLOTS FOR DRAINAGE (2 REQ'D)

2. IF TIRE IS IN HORIZONTAL POSITION

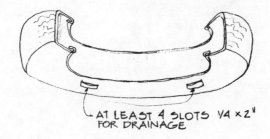

AT LEAST 4 SLOTS 1/4 × 2" FOR DRAINAGE

TYPICAL TIRE DIMENSIONS

	ID	O.D	WIDTH
13 - 155	13"	22"	6"
7.75 - 14	14"	25"	7"
8.00 - 16	16"	27"	8"
7.50 - 20	20"	35 ½"	7"
10.00 - 20	20"	41"	9"
9 - 20	20"	39"	9"
13 - 24	24"	46"	12"

55 GAL DRUM DIM.
36" HIGH × 24" DIA.

advanced tire stacking

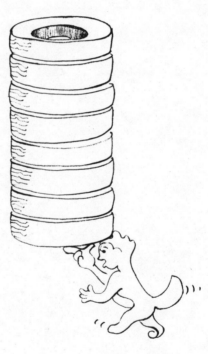

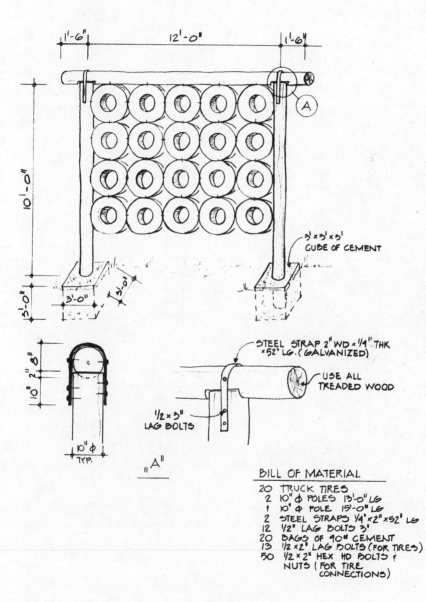

3'x3'x3'
CUBE OF CEMENT

STEEL STRAP 2" WD × 1/4" THK
×52" LG. (GALVANIZED)

USE ALL
TREADED WOOD

1/2 × 3"
LAG BOLTS

10" φ
TYP.

"A"

BILL OF MATERIAL

20 TRUCK TIRES
2 10" φ POLES 13'-0" LG
1 10" φ POLE 15'-0" LG
2 STEEL STRAPS 1/4"×2"×52" LG
12 1/2" LAG BOLTS 3'
20 BAGS OF 90# CEMENT
13 1/2 ×2" LAG BOLTS (FOR TIRES)
50 1/2 ×2" HEX HD BOLTS &
   NUTS (FOR TIRE
            CONNECTIONS)

TIRE CLIMB & FIREMAN SLIDES

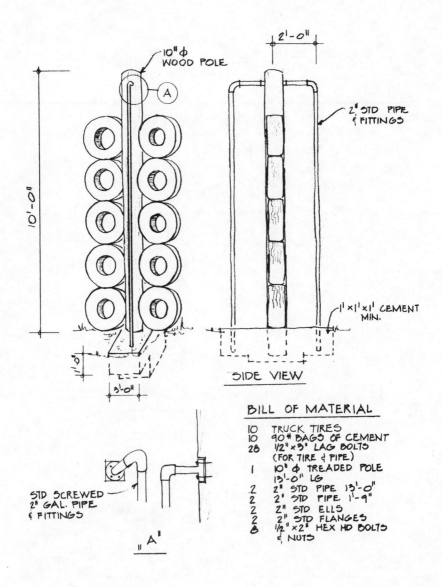

10"ϕ WOOD POLE

Ⓐ

2'-0"

2" STD PIPE & FITTINGS

10'-0"

1'x1'x1' CEMENT MIN.

3'-0"

SIDE VIEW

STD SCREWED 2" GAL. PIPE & FITTINGS

"A"

BILL OF MATERIAL

10	TRUCK TIRES
10	90# BAGS OF CEMENT
28	1/2"x3" LAG BOLTS (FOR TIRE & PIPE)
1	10"ϕ TREADED POLE 13'-0" LG
2	2" STD PIPE 13'-0"
2	2" STD PIPE 1'-9"
2	2" STD ELLS
2	2" STD FLANGES
8	1/2"x2" HEX HD BOLTS & NUTS

MONKEY TIRES
STRUCTURE I

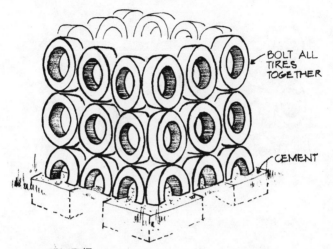

BOLT ALL
TIRES
TOGETHER

CEMENT

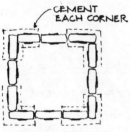

CEMENT
EACH CORNER

TOP VIEW

BILL OF MATERIAL

16 - 90# BAGS OF CEMENT
36 - TIRES
60 - 5/8 × 2" HEX HEAD
      MACHINE BOLTS w/
      WASHERS AND NUTS

MONKEY TIRES
STRUCTURE 2

BOLT ALL TIRES
TOGETHER

CEMENT
AS SHOWN

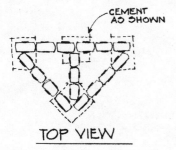

TOP VIEW

BILL OF MATERIAL

12 - 90# BAGS OF CEMENT
51 - TIRES
80 - 5/8 x 2" HEX HEAD
      MACHINE BOLTS W/
      WASHERS AND NUTS

52

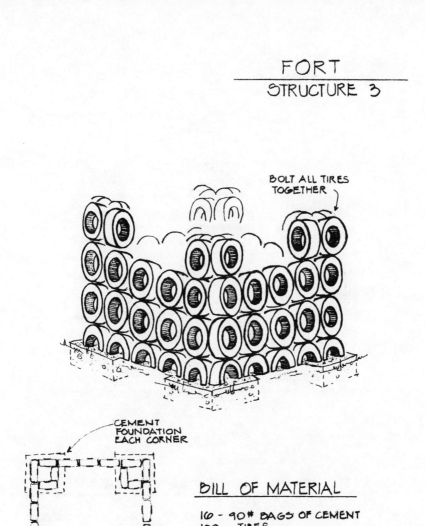

BOLT ALL TIRES
TOGETHER

CEMENT
FOUNDATION
EACH CORNER

BILL OF MATERIAL

16 - 90# BAGS OF CEMENT
100 - TIRES
170 - 5/8 x 2" HEX HEAD
MACHINE BOLTS W/
WASHERS AND NUTS

TOP VIEW

CASTLE
STRUCTURE 4

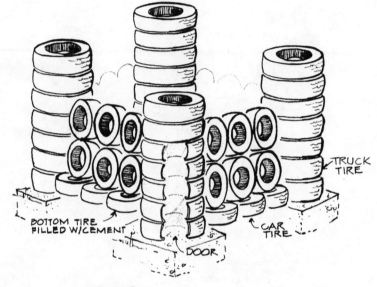

TRUCK TIRE

BOTTOM TIRE FILLED W/CEMENT

CAR TIRE

DOOR

CEMENT EACH CORNER

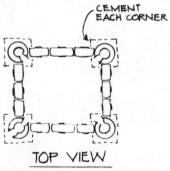

TOP VIEW

BILL OF MATERIAL

16 - 90# BAGS OF CEMENT
28 - TRUCK TIRES
36 - CAR TIRES
140 - 5/8 x 2" HEX HEAD
      MACHINE BOLTS W/
      WASHERS AND NUTS

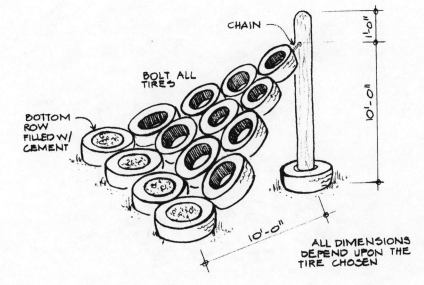

CHAIN

BOLT ALL TIRES

BOTTOM ROW FILLED W/ CEMENT

1'-0"

10'-0"

10'-0"

ALL DIMENSIONS DEPEND UPON THE TIRE CHOSEN

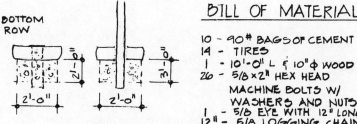

BOTTOM ROW

2'-0"

2'-0"

3'-0"

2'-0"

BILL OF MATERIAL

10 - 90# BAGS OF CEMENT
14 - TIRES
1 - 10'-0" L & 10"∅ WOOD POLE
26 - 5/8 x 2" HEX HEAD
     MACHINE BOLTS W/
     WASHERS AND NUTS
1 - 5/8 EYE WITH 12" LONG SHANK
12" - 5/8 LOGGING CHAIN

TREE-TO
STRUCTURE 6

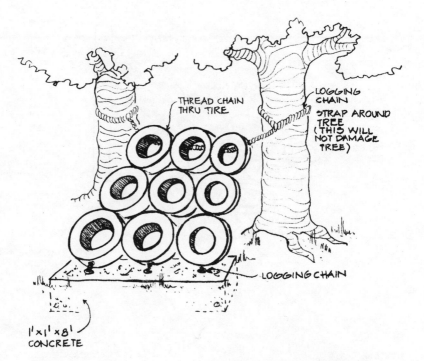

THREAD CHAIN THRU TIRE

LOGGING CHAIN

STRAP AROUND TREE
(THIS WILL NOT DAMAGE TREE)

LOGGING CHAIN

1'x1'x8'
CONCRETE

BILL OF MATERIAL

(2) TREES 10" ∅ OR LARGER
9 - 90# BAGS OF CEMENT
9 - TIRES
12 - 5/8 x 2" HEX HEAD BOLTS,
      WASHERS AND NUTS
3 PCS 18" LOGGING CHAIN
      5/8" THICK
1 PC 5/8" LOGGING CHAIN
      CUT TO LENGTH FOR TREES

FULL LEAN-TO
STRUCTURE 7

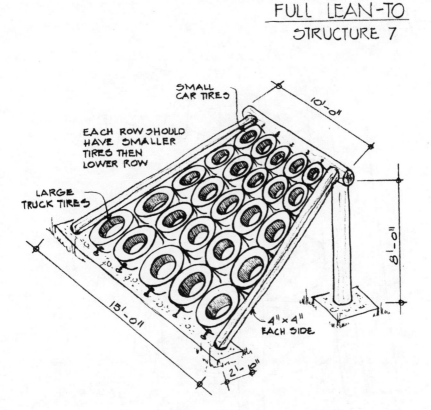

SMALL CAR TIRES

EACH ROW SHOULD HAVE SMALLER TIRES THEN LOWER ROW

LARGE TRUCK TIRES

10'-0"

8'-0"

15'-0"

2'-0"

4" x 4" EACH SIDE

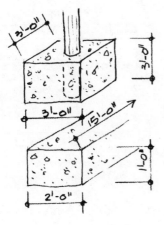

3'-0"

3'-0"

3'-0"

3'-0"

15'-0"

2'-0"

1'-0"

BILL OF MATERIAL

22	-	90# BAGS OF CEMENT
1	-	10" ∅ WOOD POLE 10'-0" LONG
2	-	10" ∅ WOOD POLE 11'-0" LONG
2	-	4" x 4" WOOD POLE
25	-	VARIOUS SIZE TIRES
10	PCS	12" x 5/8 ∅ LOGGING CHAIN
50	-	5/8 x 2" HEX HEAD MACHINE BOLTS w/ WASHERS AND NUTS

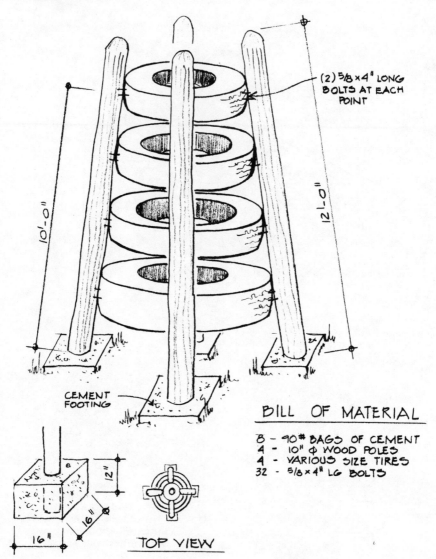

(2) 5/8 × 4" LONG BOLTS AT EACH POINT

10'-0"

12'-0"

CEMENT FOOTING

12"

16"   16"

TOP VIEW

BILL OF MATERIAL

8 - 90# BAGS OF CEMENT
4 - 10" Ø WOOD POLES
4 - VARIOUS SIZE TIRES
32 - 5/8 × 4" LG BOLTS

58

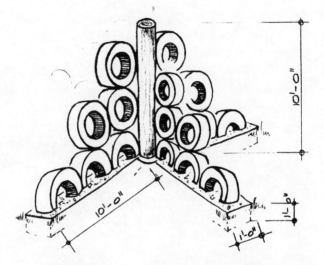

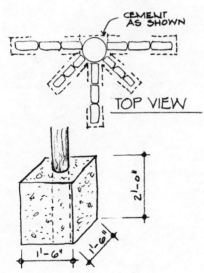

CEMENT AS SHOWN

TOP VIEW

BILL OF MATERIAL

25 - 90# BAGS OF CEMENT
30 - VARIOUS SIZE TIRES
1 - 10" ∅ WOOD POLE
35 - 5/8 x 2" HEX HEAD
     MACHINE BOLTS w/
     WASHERS AND NUTS
15 - 5/8 x 4" LG BOLTS

10'-0"

10'-0"

1'-0"

1'-0"

2'-0"

1'-6"

1'-6"

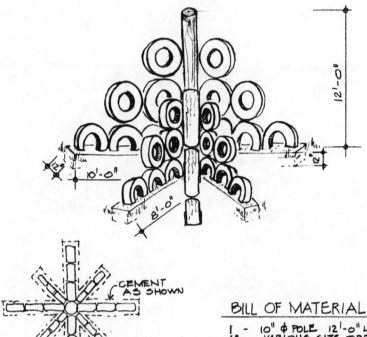

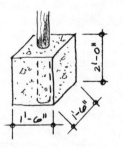

CEMENT
AS SHOWN

TOP VIEW

BILL OF MATERIAL

1 - 10" ⌀ POLE 12'-0" LG
48 - VARIOUS SIZE TIRES
35 - 90# BAGS OF CEMENT
48 - 5/8 x 2" HEX HEAD
      MACHINE BOLTS W/
      WASHERS AND NUTS

24 - 5/8 x 4" LG BOLTS

60

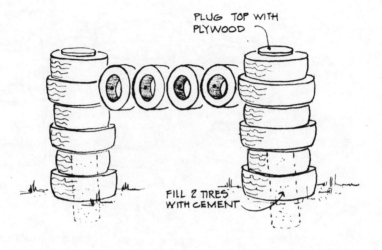

PLUG TOP WITH
PLYWOOD

FILL 2 TIRES
WITH CEMENT

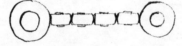

TOP VIEW

SEE DETAIL
PAGE

BILL OF MATERIAL

6 CAR TIRES
6 SMALLER CAR TIRES
4 SMALL TIRES
6 90 # BAGS OF CEMENT
50 3/8 x 2" HEX HD BOLTS &
                     NUTS

BRIDGE

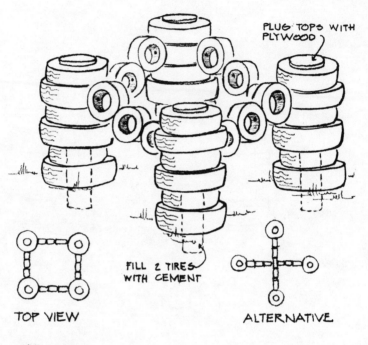

PLUG TOPS WITH PLYWOOD

FILL 2 TIRES WITH CEMENT

TOP VIEW

SEE DETAIL PAGE

ALTERNATIVE

BILL OF MATERIAL

12	CAR TIRES
12	SMALLER CAR TIRES
12	SMALL TIRES
12	90 # BAGS OF CEMENT
100	5/8 X 2" HEX HD BOLT & NUTS

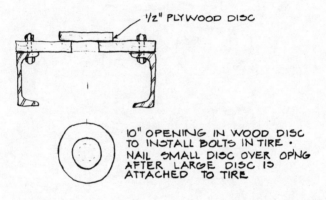

½" PLYWOOD DISC

10" OPENING IN WOOD DISC
TO INSTALL BOLTS IN TIRE ·
NAIL SMALL DISC OVER OP'NG
AFTER LARGE DISC IS
ATTACHED TO TIRE

MONKEY APARTMENT

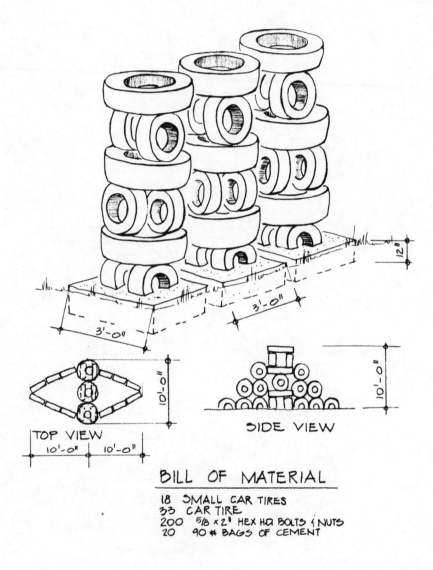

TOP VIEW
10'-0" | 10'-0"

SIDE VIEW

BILL OF MATERIAL

18 SMALL CAR TIRES
33 CAR TIRE
200 5/8 x 2" HEX HD BOLTS & NUTS
20 90 # BAGS OF CEMENT

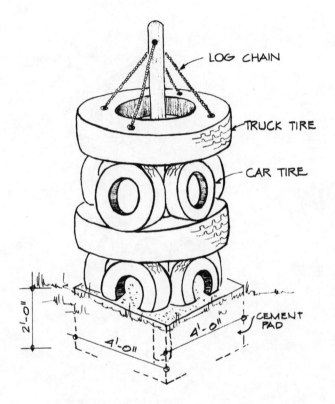

LOG CHAIN

TRUCK TIRE

CAR TIRE

CEMENT PAD

2'-0"

4'-0"

4'-0"

BILL OF MATERIAL

2   LARGE TRUCK TIRES
8   CAR TIRES
4 PIECES 1/2" LOG CHAIN × 4'-0" LG
4   1/2" × 4" EYE BOLTS
8   90 # BAGS OF CEMENT
20 1/2" × 2" BOLTS WITH HEX
      NUTS AND WASHERS
1 10" Φ TREADED WOOD POLE

PLATFORM # 2

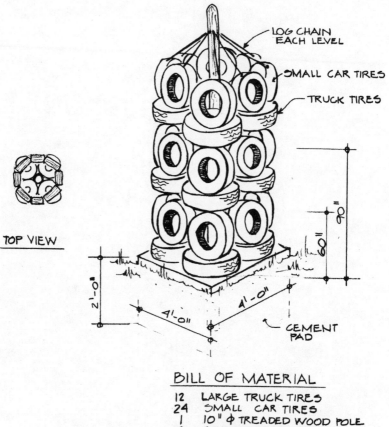

LOG CHAIN
EACH LEVEL

SMALL CAR TIRES

TRUCK TIRES

TOP VIEW

60"

90"

2'-0"

4'-0"

4'-0"

CEMENT
PAD

BILL OF MATERIAL

12   LARGE TRUCK TIRES
24   SMALL CAR TIRES
 1   10" ⌀ TREADED WOOD POLE
 8   90# BAGS OF CEMENT
60   1/2" x 2" BOLTS WITH HEX NUTS
     AND WASHERS
12   1/2" x 3" LOG BOLTS
 8   1/2" x 4" LOG EYES
 8 PIECES 1/2 LOGGING CHAIN
     x 4'-0" LONG

TIRE TREE #1

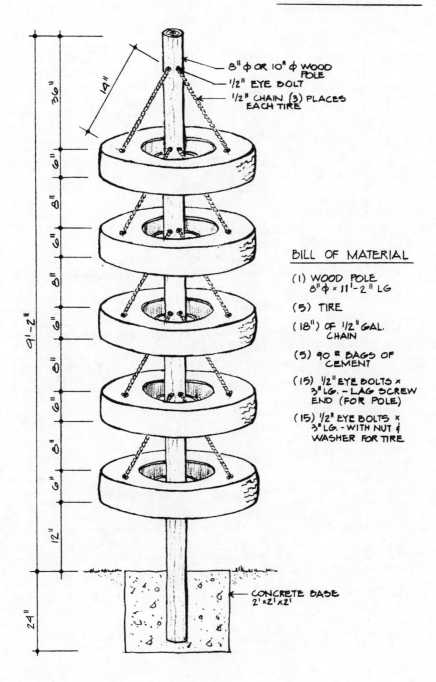

8" φ OR 10" φ WOOD POLE
1/2" EYE BOLT
1/2" CHAIN (3) PLACES EACH TIRE

14"

36"

6"

8"

6"

8"

6"

6"

6"

6"

9'-2"

12"

24"

CONCRETE BASE
2' x 2' x 2'

BILL OF MATERIAL

(1) WOOD POLE
   8" φ x 11' - 2" LG

(5) TIRE

(18") OF 1/2" GAL. CHAIN

(5) 90 # BAGS OF CEMENT

(15) 1/2" EYE BOLTS x
   3" LG. - LAG SCREW
   END (FOR POLE)

(15) 1/2" EYE BOLTS x
   3" LG. - WITH NUT &
   WASHER FOR TIRE

TIRE TREE #2

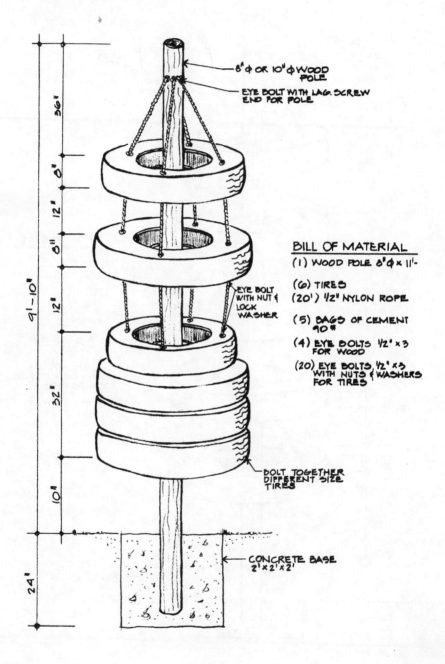

8" ∅ OR 10" ∅ WOOD POLE

EYE BOLT WITH LAG. SCREW END FOR POLE

36"

8"

12"

8"

12"

9'-10"

EYE BOLT WITH NUT & LOCK WASHER

32"

10"

BOLT TOGETHER DIFFERENT SIZE TIRES

24"

CONCRETE BASE 2' x 2' x 2'

BILL OF MATERIAL

(1) WOOD POLE 8"∅ x 11'-

(6) TIRES

(20') 1/2" NYLON ROPE

(5) BAGS OF CEMENT 90 #

(4) EYE BOLTS 1/2" x 3 FOR WOOD

(20) EYE BOLTS 1/2" x 3 WITH NUTS & WASHERS FOR TIRES

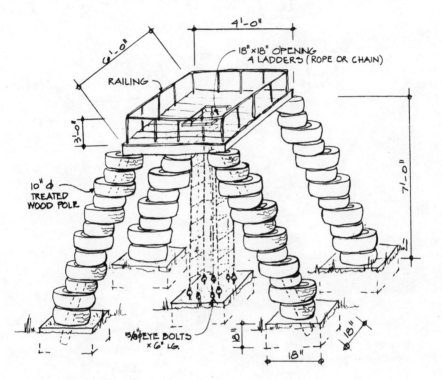

4'-0"

6'-0"

18"×18" OPENING
4 LADDERS (ROPE OR CHAIN)

RAILING

3'-0"

7'-0"

10" ⌀ TREATED WOOD POLE

5/8 ⌀ EYE BOLTS × 6" LG.

18"

18"

18"

BILL OF MATERIAL

48	TIRES- VARIOUS SIZE
12	90 # BAGS OF CEMENT
200	5/8 × 2" HEX HD BOLTS & NUTS
8	5/8 ⌀ EYE BOLTS 6" LG
4	4" × 4" × 6' LG TREATED WOOD
2	4" × 4" × 4' LG " "
12	1/2" × 6" × 4' LG " "
	MISC. NUTS

moving tires

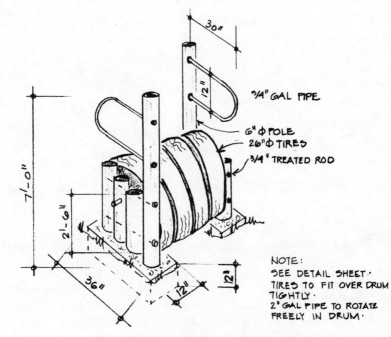

3/4" GAL PIPE

6" Ø POLE
26" Ø TIRES
3/4" TREATED ROD

NOTE:
SEE DETAIL SHEET ·
TIRES TO FIT OVER DRUM
TIGHTLY ·
2" GAL PIPE TO ROTATE
FREELY IN DRUM ·

BILL OF MATERIAL

(4) 26" TIRES
(2) 3/4" SCH 40 GAL PIPE × 84" LG
(4) 3/4" TREATED ROD × 27" LG
(8) 3/4 HEX NUTS AND FLAT WASHERS
(2) 6" Ø TREATED WOOD POLES × 96" LG
(6) 6" Ø   "   "   "   × 42"
(6) 90# BAGS OF CEMENT
(2) 1" THK × 8" × 8" TREATED WOOD
(4) 2" × 6" TREATED WOOD × 48"
     CUT TO FIT TIRES
(1) 2" SCH 40 PIPE × 60"

DETAILS
TIRE ROLL

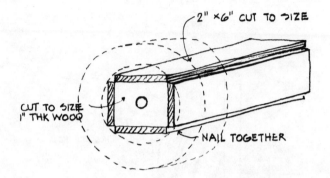

2" ×6" CUT TO SIZE

CUT TO SIZE
1" THK WOOD

NAIL TOGETHER

TIRES TO FIT OVER DRUM TIGHTLY
2" GAL PIPE TO ROTATE FREELY IN DRUM

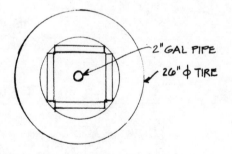

2" GAL PIPE

26" φ TIRE

TIRE ON SPRING

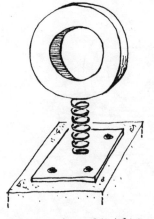

VERTICAL SINGLE

BILL OF MATERIAL

(1) TIRE
(1) TRUCK SPRING
(1) 1/4" PLATE 12"×12"
(4) ANCHOR BOLTS
(2) 90# BAGS OF CEMENT

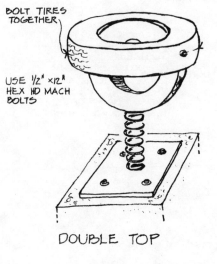

BOLT TIRES
TOGETHER

USE 1/2"×12"
HEX HD MACH
BOLTS

DOUBLE TOP

BILL OF MATERIAL

(2) TIRES
(1) TRUCK SPRING
(1) 1/4" PLATE 12"×12"
(4) ANCHOR BOLTS
(2) 90# BAGS OF CEMENT
(2) BOLTS AS SHOWN

TIRE ON SPRING 2

BOLT TOGETHER
WITH 5/8" x 12"
HEX HD BOLTS

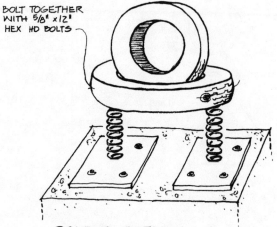

DOUBLE BOTTOM

BILL OF MATERIAL

(2) TIRES
(2) TRUCK SPRINGS
(2) 1/4" PLATE 12" x 12"
(8) ANCHOR BOLTS
(4) 90# BAGS OF CEMENT
(2) BOLTS AS SHOWN

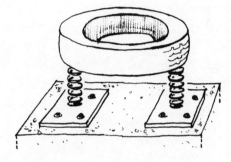

BILL OF MATERIAL

(1) TIRE
(2) TRUCK SPRINGS
(2) 1/4" PLATE 12" x 12"
(8) ANCHOR BOLTS
(4) 90# BAGS OF CEMENT

HORIZONTAL SINGLE

BILL OF MATERIAL

(3) TIRES
(2) TRUCK SPRINGS
(2) 1/4" PLATE 12" x 12"
(8) ANCHOR BOLTS
(4) BAGS OF CEMENT, 90#
(4) BOLTS AS SHOWN

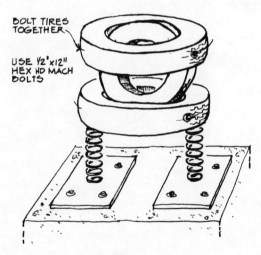

BOLT TIRES TOGETHER

USE 1/2"x12" HEX HD MACH BOLTS

TRIPLE

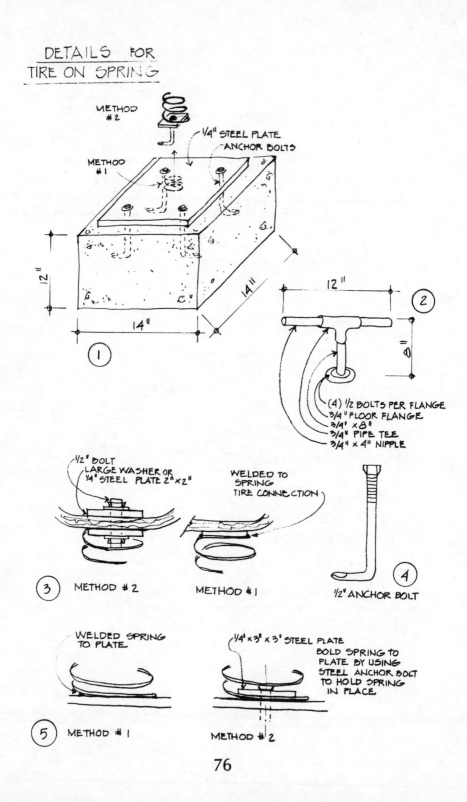

DETAILS FOR TIRE ON SPRING

METHOD #2

1/4" STEEL PLATE
ANCHOR BOLTS

METHOD #1

12"

14"

14"

①

12"

8"

②

(4) 1/2 BOLTS PER FLANGE
3/4" FLOOR FLANGE
3/4" × 8"
3/4" PIPE TEE
3/4" × 4" NIPPLE

1/2" BOLT
LARGE WASHER OR
1/4" STEEL PLATE 2" × 2"

WELDED TO
SPRING
TIRE CONNECTION

③ METHOD #2

METHOD #1

1/2" ANCHOR BOLT

④

WELDED SPRING
TO PLATE

1/4" × 3" × 3" STEEL PLATE
BOLD SPRING TO
PLATE BY USING
STEEL ANCHOR BOLT
TO HOLD SPRING
IN PLACE

⑤ METHOD #1

METHOD #2

76

SEE-SAW ON TIRE

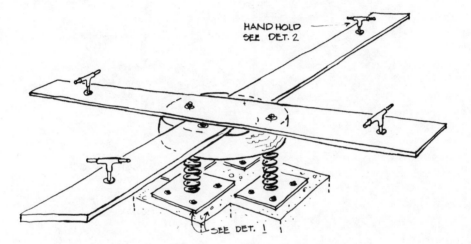

HAND HOLD
SEE DET. 2

SEE DET. 1

BILL OF MATERIAL

(1) LARGE TRUCK TIRE
(4) TRUCK SPRINGS
(4) ¼" PLATE 12" x 12"
(16) ANCHOR BOLTS
(2) 2" x 8" x 10'-0" TREATED
         LUMBER
(4) HAND HOLDS
(8) 90# BAGS OF CEMENT
(4) BOLTS

PLATFORM SEE-SAW

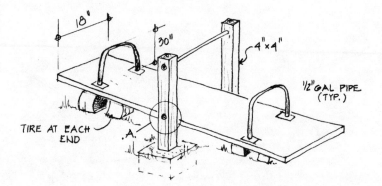

18"

30"

4"×4"

½" GAL PIPE
(TYP.)

TIRE AT EACH
END

.A.

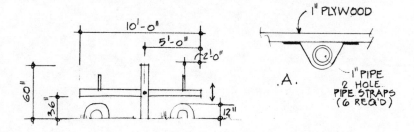

10'-0"

5'-0"

2'-0"

60"

36"

12"

1" PLYWOOD

.A.

1" PIPE
2 HOLE
PIPE STRAPS
(6 REQ'D)

BILL OF MATERIAL

(1) EXTERIOR PLYWOOD 10'-0" × 18"
(6) PIPE STRAPS × 2 HOLE
(2) 1" ⌀ PIPE × 26" LG
(2) TIRES
(6) 90# BAGS OF CEMENT
(2) ½" GAL PIPE × 80"
(2) 4" × 4" TREATED WOOD × 72"

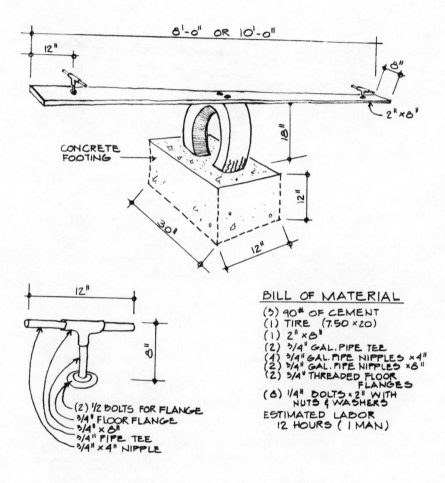

8'-0" OR 10'-0"

12"

8"

2" × 8"

18"

CONCRETE
FOOTING

30"

12"

12"

12"

8"

(2) 1/2 BOLTS FOR FLANGE
3/4" FLOOR FLANGE
3/4" × 8"
3/4" PIPE TEE
3/4" × 4" NIPPLE

BILL OF MATERIAL

(3) 90# OF CEMENT
(1) TIRE (7.50 × 20)
(1) 2" × 8"
(2) 3/4" GAL. PIPE TEE
(4) 3/4" GAL. PIPE NIPPLES × 4"
(2) 3/4" GAL. PIPE NIPPLES × 8"
(2) 3/4" THREADED FLOOR
                    FLANGES
(8) 1/4" BOLTS × 2" WITH
        NUTS & WASHERS
ESTIMATED LABOR
    12 HOURS (1 MAN)

DOUBLE SEE-SAW

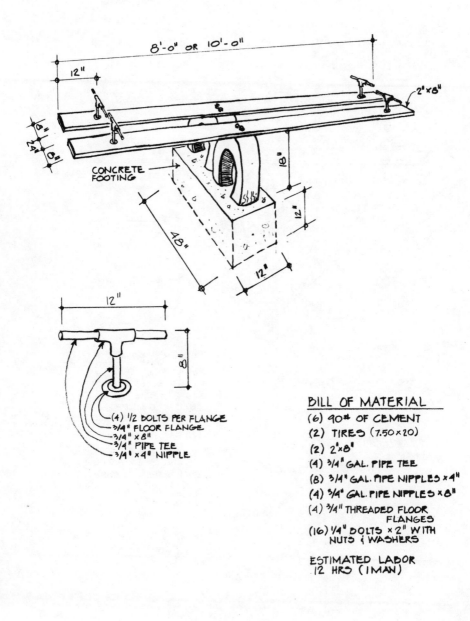

8'-0" OR 10'-0"

12"

2"x8"

4"
24"
8"

CONCRETE
FOOTING

18"

12"

48"

12"

12"

8"

(4) 1/2 BOLTS PER FLANGE
3/4" FLOOR FLANGE
3/4" x 8"
3/4" PIPE TEE
3/4" x 4" NIPPLE

BILL OF MATERIAL

(6) 90# OF CEMENT
(2) TIRES (7.50 x 20)
(2) 2"x8"
(4) 3/4" GAL. PIPE TEE
(8) 3/4" GAL. PIPE NIPPLES x 4"
(4) 3/4" GAL. PIPE NIPPLES x 8"
(4) 3/4" THREADED FLOOR
           FLANGES
(16) 1/4" BOLTS x 2" WITH
         NUTS & WASHERS

ESTIMATED LABOR
12 HRS (1 MAN)

AND

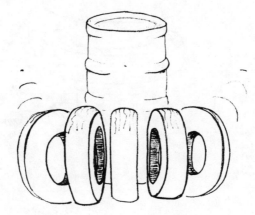

DRUM TIRE POLE

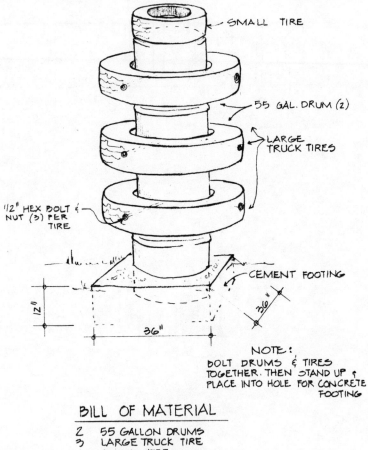

SMALL TIRE

55 GAL. DRUM (2)

LARGE TRUCK TIRES

1/2" HEX BOLT &
NUT (3) PER
TIRE

CEMENT FOOTING

12"

36"

36"

NOTE:
BOLT DRUMS & TIRES
TOGETHER. THEN STAND UP &
PLACE INTO HOLE FOR CONCRETE
FOOTING

BILL OF MATERIAL

2   55 GALLON DRUMS
3   LARGE TRUCK TIRE
1   SMALL TIRE
9   1/2" BOLTS & NUTS - LENGTH
    AS REQ'D
4   90# BAGS OF CEMENT

RYDER DRUM

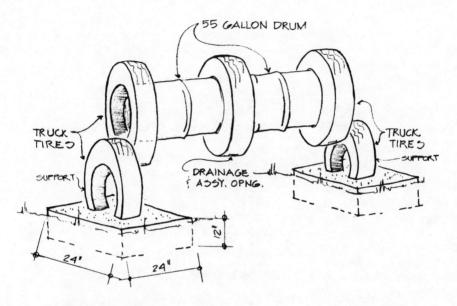

55 GALLON DRUM

TRUCK TIRES

SUPPORT

DRAINAGE & ASSY. OPNG.

TRUCK TIRES

SUPPORT

12"

24'

24"

SEE FOLLOWING
DETAIL PAGE

BILL OF MATERIAL

5   TRUCK TIRES
2   DRUMS
16 5/8 x 2" HEX HD. BOLTS & NUTS
4   90 # BAGS OF CEMENT

83

METHOD OF ASSEMBLY - USE OPEN-TOP DRUM

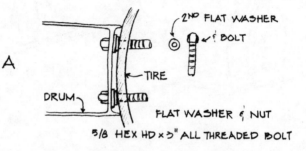

A

2ND FLAT WASHER

& BOLT

TIRE

DRUM

FLAT WASHER & NUT

5/8 HEX HD x 5" ALL THREADED BOLT

B   BOLT TIRE TO DRUM TOP, ATTACH TOP & DRUM RING TO DRUM, WELD RING ONTO DRUM

C   INSTALL BETWEEN SUPPORT TIRES

MOVING TUNNEL

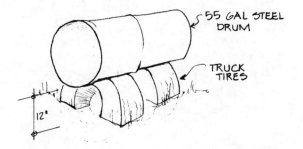

55 GAL STEEL DRUM

TRUCK TIRES

12"

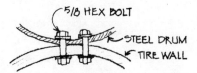

5/8 HEX BOLT

STEEL DRUM

TIRE WALL

BILL OF MATERIAL

(1) 55 GAL DRUM - CUT BOLT ENDS
OUT & GRIND SMOOTH
(2) TRUCK TIRES
(4) 5/8 HEX BOLT, WASHERS & NUTS

swinging tires

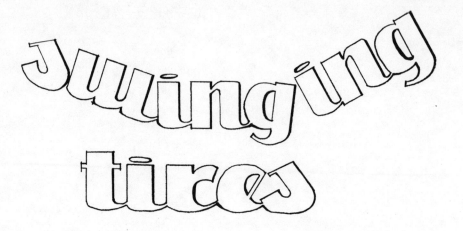

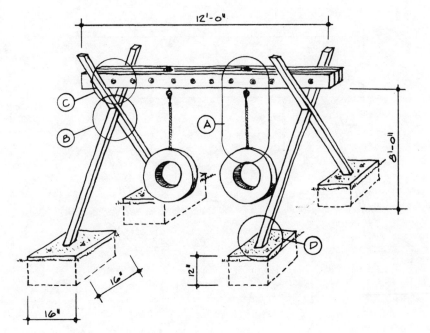

BILL OF MATERIAL

(2) TIRES
(4) 4" x 4" x 12'-0" LG TREATED
(3) 2" x 6" x 12'-0" LG TREATED
(2) 5/8 EYE BOLT
(12) 5/8 x 8" BOLTS, NUTS &
                         WASHERS
(7) 90# BAGS OF CEMENT
8' 3/4" NYLON ROPE

TRIPLE SWING

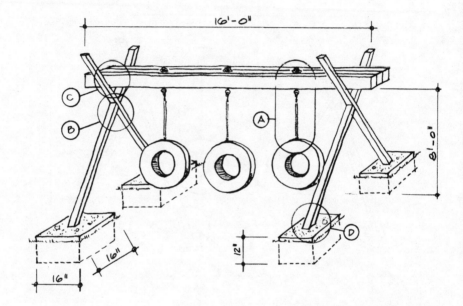

16'-0"

8'-0"

12"

16"

16"

A

B

C

D

BILL OF MATERIAL
- (3) TIRES
- (4) 4"x4"x12'-0" LG TREATED
- (3) 2x6"x16'-0" LG TREATED
- (3) 5/8 EYE BOLT
- (16) 5/8 x 8" BOLTS, NUTS & WASHERS
- (7) 90# BAGS OF CEMENT
- 12' 3/4" Ø NYLON ROPE

QUAD. SWING

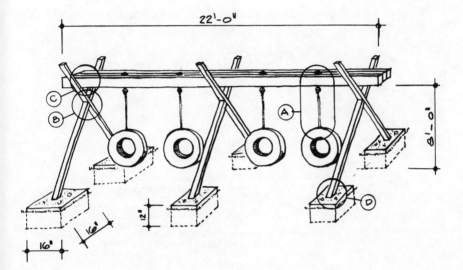

22'-0"

8'-0"

12"

16"

16"

BILL OF MATERIAL

(4) TIRES
(6) 4" × 4" × 12'-0" LG TREATED
(3) 2" × 6" × 22'-0" LG TREATED
(4) 5/8 EYE BOLT
(22) 5/8 × 8" BOLTS { NUTS {
               WASHERS
(11) 90# BAGS OF CEMENT
16' 3/4" NYLON ROPE

DOUBLE SWING & SPIDER CLIMB (5)

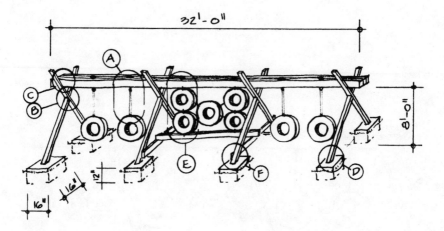

BILL OF MATERIAL
(9) TIRES
(6) 4" × 4" × 12'-0" LG TREATED
(6) 2" × 6" × 16'-0" LG TREATED, BOLTED
(6) 5/8 EYE BOLTS   TOGETHER
(30) 5/8 × 8" BOLTS, NUTS &
          WASHERS
(16) 90# BAGS OF CEMENT
20' 3/4" NYLON ROPE
(2) 2" × 6' × 10'-0"
(3) 2" × 6" × 12'-0"

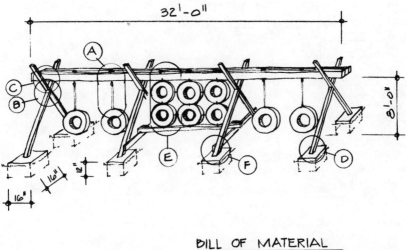

BILL OF MATERIAL

(10) TIRES
(8) 4"×4"×12'-0" LG TREATED
(6) 2"×6"×16'-0" LG TREATED, BOLTED TOGETHER
(7) EYE BOLTS 5/8
(30) 5/8×8" BOLTS, NUTS & WASHERS
(16) 90# BAGS OF CEMENT
22'-0" 3/4" NYLON ROPE
(2) 2"×6"×10'-0"
(3) 2"×6"×12'-0"

SWING DETAILS

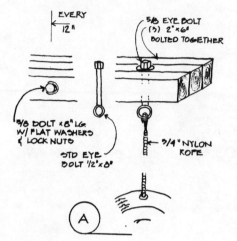

EVERY 12"

5/8 EYE BOLT
(3) 2"×6"
BOLTED TOGETHER

3/8 BOLT ×8" LG
W/ FLAT WASHERS
& LOCK NUTS

STD EYE
BOLT 1/2"×8"

3/4" NYLON
ROPE

(A)

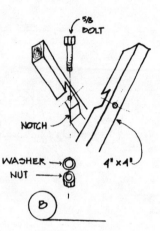

5/8
BOLT

NOTCH

WASHER →

NUT →

4"×4"

(B)

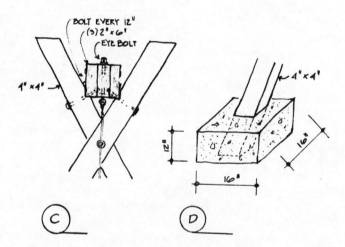

BOLT EVERY 12"
(3) 2"×6"
EYE BOLT

4"×4"

4"×4"

12"

16"

16"

(C)

(D)

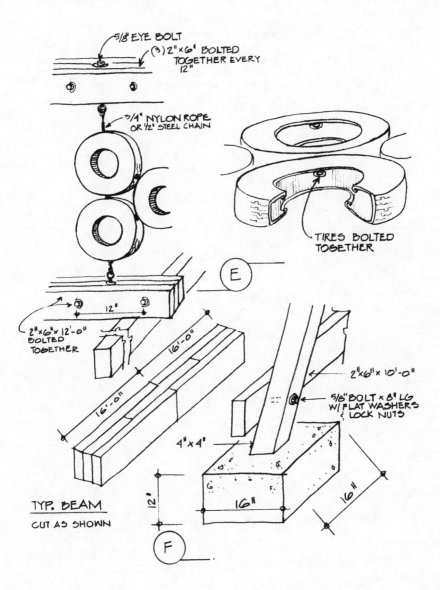

5/8" EYE BOLT

(3) 2"x6' BOLTED TOGETHER EVERY 12"

3/4" NYLON ROPE OR 1/2" STEEL CHAIN

TIRES BOLTED TOGETHER

E

12"

2"x6"x12'-0" BOLTED TOGETHER

16'-0"

16'-0"

16'-0"

2"x6"x10'-0"

5/8" BOLT x 8" LG W/ FLAT WASHERS & LOCK NUTS

4"x4"

12"

16"

16"

TYP. BEAM
CUT AS SHOWN

F

ANIMALS AND THINGS

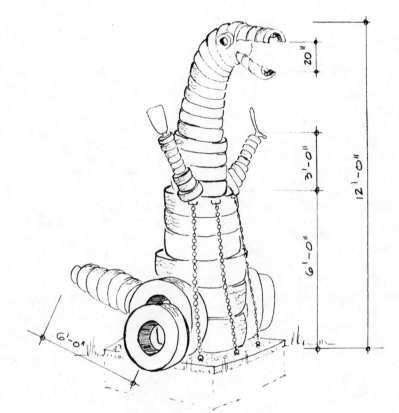

BILL OF MATERIAL

5	TRACTOR TIRES
5	LARGE TRUCK TIRES
4	CAR TIRES
41	VARIOUS SIZE TIRES
25	90# BAGS OF CEMENT
20'	1/2" LOGGING CHAIN
40'	2" GAL. PIPE
100	3/8 × 2" HEX BOLTS & NUTS

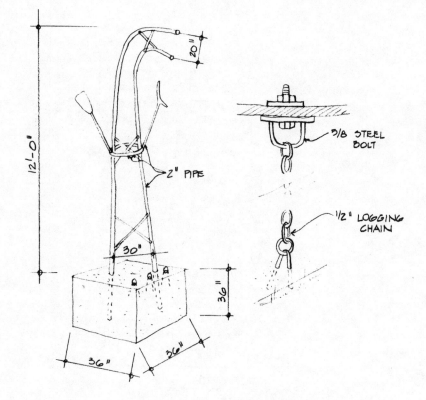

20"

12'-0"

2" PIPE

30"

36"

36"

36"

5/8 STEEL BOLT

1/2" LOGGING CHAIN

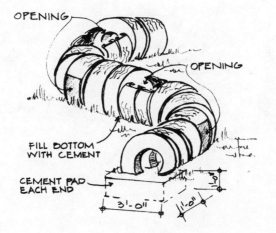

OPENING

OPENING

FILL BOTTOM
WITH CEMENT

CEMENT PAD
EACH END

3'-0"

1'-0"

BILL OF MATERIAL

16   CAR TIRES
32   1/2" x 2" BOLTS WITH
       HEX NUTS AND WASHERS
4   40 # BAGS OF CEMENT

DRAGON

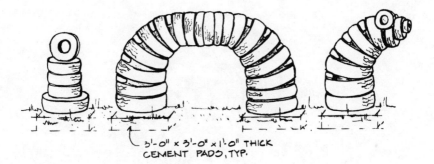

3'-0" x 3'-0" x 1'-0" THICK
CEMENT PADS, TYP.

BILL OF MATERIAL

40   TIRES OF VARIOUS SIZES
24   90# BAGS OF CEMENT
120   1/2" x 2" BOLTS, HEX NUTS
       AND WASHERS

NOTE: THIS IS TO CLIMB ON ONLY,
         NOT TO PLAY INSIDE OF

SEA HORSE

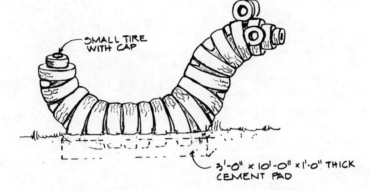

SMALL TIRE
WITH CAP

3'-0" x 10'-0" x 1'-0" THICK
CEMENT PAD

BILL OF MATERIAL

24	VARIOUS SIZE TIRES
20	90# BAGS OF CEMENT
72	1/2" x 2" BOLTS, HEX NUTS AND WASHERS

NOTE: THIS IS TO CLIMB ON ONLY,
NOT TO PLAY INSIDE OF

SEAL

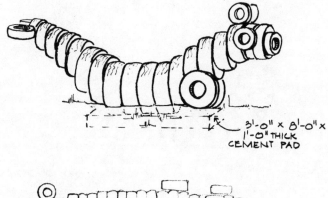

3'-0" x 8'-0" x 1'-0" THICK CEMENT PAD

TOP VIEW

BILL OF MATERIAL

26 TIRES, VARIOUS SIZE
20 90# BAGS OF CEMENT
78 1/2" x 2" BOLTS, HEX NUTS
    AND WASHERS

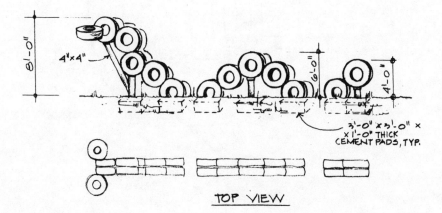

8'-0"

4"x4"

6'-0"

4'-0"

3'-0" x 3'-0" x
x 1'-0" THICK
CEMENT PADS, TYP.

TOP VIEW

BILL OF MATERIAL

20	90# BAGS OF CEMENT
26	TIRES - SAME SIZE
52	1/2" x 2" BOLTS, HEX NUTS AND WASHERS
4	PIECES AT 4" x 4" TREADED WOOD, LENGTH TO SUIT TIRE SIZE

CHARIOT 1

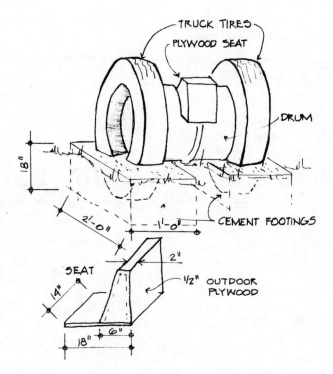

TRUCK TIRES
PLYWOOD SEAT
DRUM
18"
2'-0"
1'-0"
CEMENT FOOTINGS
SEAT
2"
1/2" OUTDOOR PLYWOOD
14"
18"
6"

BILL OF MATERIAL

2	TRUCK TIRES
1	55 GAL DRUM
4	90 # BAGS OF CEMENT
1	4' ×8' × 1/2" THICK SHEET OF OUTDOOR PLYWOOD

CHARIOT 2

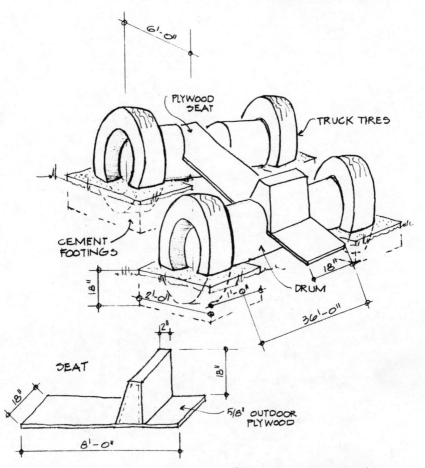

6'-0"

PLYWOOD
SEAT

TRUCK TIRES

CEMENT
FOOTINGS

18"

2'-0"

1'-0"

DRUM

18"

36'-0"

SEAT

2"

18"

18"

5/8" OUTDOOR
PLYWOOD

8'-0"

BILL OF MATERIAL

4   TRUCK TIRES
2   55 GALLON DRUMS
1   5/8" x 4' x 8' OUTDOOR PLYWOOD
18   5/8" x 2" HEX HD BOLT & NUTS
8   90# BAGS OF CEMENT

ROCKET

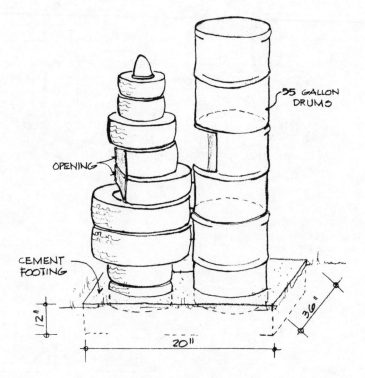

55 GALLON DRUMS

OPENING

CEMENT FOOTING

12"

3'6"

20"

BILL OF MATERIAL

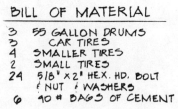

3	55 GALLON DRUMS
3	CAR TIRES
4	SMALLER TIRES
2	SMALL TIRES
24	5/8" X 2" HEX. HD. BOLT
	& NUT & WASHERS
6	90 # BAGS OF CEMENT

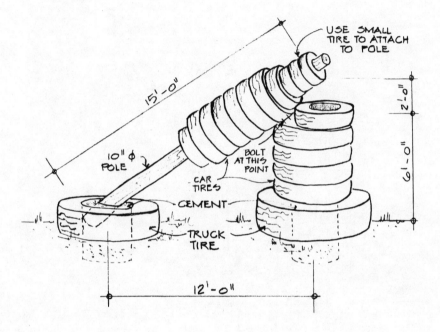

USE SMALL
TIRE TO ATTACH
TO POLE

15'-0"

2'-0"

6'-0"

10" φ
POLE

BOLT
AT THIS
POINT

CAR
TIRES

CEMENT

TRUCK
TIRE

12'-0"

BILL OF MATERIAL

2   TRUCK TIRES
10 + 3   CAR TIRES
3   SMALL CARE TIRE
8   90# BAGS OF CEMENT
50   5/8 × 2" HEX HD BOLT & NUTS

WAGON

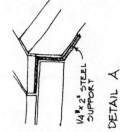

DETAIL A

1/4" x 2" STEEL SUPPORT

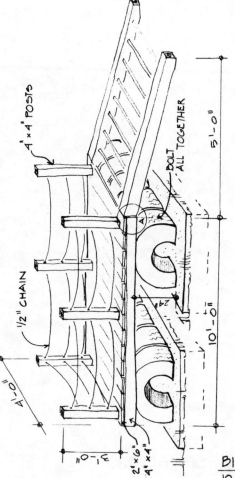

4" x 4" POSTS

BOLT ALL TOGETHER

1/2" CHAIN

5'-0"

10'-0"

24"

4'-0"

3'-0"

2" x 6"
4" x 4"

BILL OF MATERIAL

10	TIRES
8	90# BAGS OF CEMENT
6	4"x4" x36" LG WOOD
75'	1/2" CHAIN
2	4"x4" x10' LG WOOD
20	2"x6" x4' LG WOOD
2	4"x4" x 5' LG WOOD
8	48"LG x 1"⌀ PIPE
20	5/8 x2"HEX HD BOLTS & NUTS

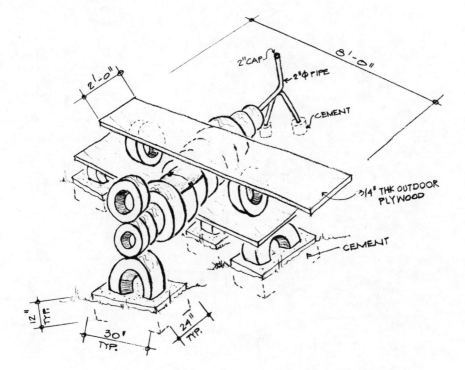

2" CAP

2" Φ PIPE

CEMENT

8'-0"

2'-0"

3/4" THK OUTDOOR PLYWOOD

CEMENT

12" TYP.

30" TYP.

24" TYP.

BILL OF MATERIAL

1 PC 3/4" x 4' x 8' OUTDOOR PLYWOOD
6 90 # BAGS OF CEMENT
6 SMALL CAR TIRES
14 LARGE CAR TIRES
60 5/8 x 2" HEX HD BOLTS & NUTS

STAGE COACH

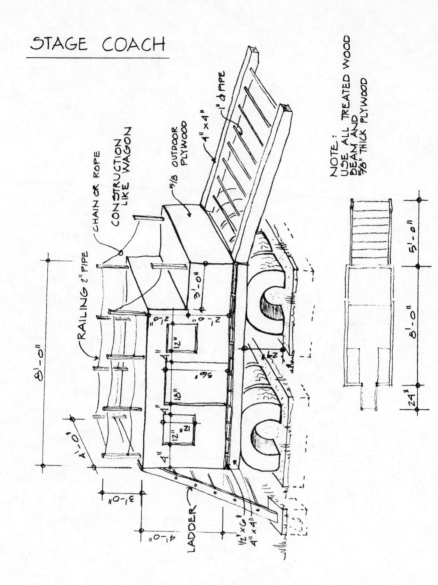

NOTE:
USE ALL TREATED WOOD
BEAM AND
⅝" THICK PLYWOOD

1" φ PIPE

4" × 4"

⅝ OUTDOOR PLYWOOD

CONSTRUCTION LIKE WAGON

CHAIN OR ROPE

RAILING 2" PIPE

8'-0"

4'-0"

3'-0"

4'-0"

3'-0"

2'-0"

2'-0"

12"

18"

36"

12"

12"

4"

LADDER

½" × 6"
4" × 4"

5'-0"

8'-0"

24"

BILL OF MATERIAL
```
 4  ⅝" × 4' × 8' OUTDOOR PLYWOOD
10  TIRES
 8  90 # BAGS OF CEMENT
10  36" LG 2" φ PIPE
26'  ½" LOGGING CHAIN
 8  48" LG × 1" φ PIPE
 6  24" LG × 1" φ PIPE
     LUMBER & NAILS TO SUIT
```

CHRISTMAS TREE

TOP VIEW

EACH TIRE IS
SMALLER THAN
ONE BELOW

LOG CHAIN

12'-0"

BILL OF MATERIAL

12	90# BAGS OF CEMENT
6	14'-0" PCS 1/2" LOGGING CHAIN
12	1/2" x 6" EYE BOLTS
24	VARIOUS SIZES TIRES
42	1/2" x 2" BOLTS WITH HEX HEAD NUTS AND FLAT WASHERS
1	10" Ø x 15'-0" WOOD POLE

109

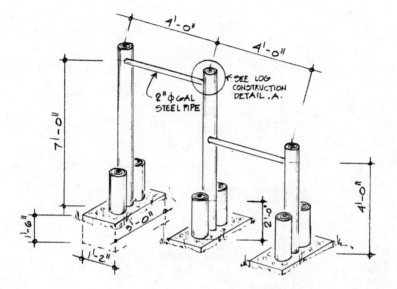

2" φ GAL STEEL PIPE

← SEE LOG CONSTRUCTION DETAIL .A.

BILL OF MATERIAL

(2) 8" φ TREATED WOOD POLES 8'-0" LG

(1) 8" φ " " 5'-0" LG "

(6) 8" φ " " 3'-0" LG "

(24) 90# BAGS OF READY MIX CEMENT

(2) 2" φ GAL STEEL PIPE SCH 40 4'-2" LG

(4) 5/8 LAG BOLTS x 6" LG

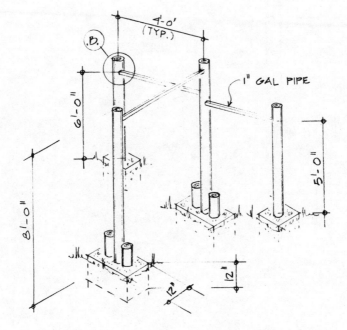

BILL OF MATERIAL

(2) 8" ⌀ TREATED WOOD POLE × 10'-0" LG
(4) 8" ⌀   "   "   " × 2'-0"   "
(2) 8" ⌀   "   "   " × 8'-0"   "
(2) 8" ⌀   "   "   " × 6'-0"   "
(20) 90 # BAGS OF READY MIX CEMENT
(3) 1" GAL SCH 40 PIPE × 50" LONG

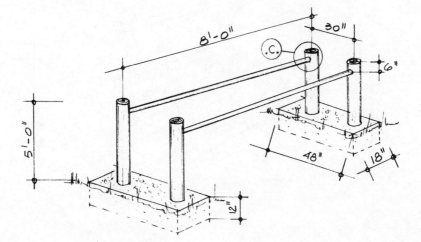

BILL OF MATERIAL

(4) 8" ⌀ TREATED WOOD POLE x 6'-0"
(2) 2" SCH 40 GAL PIPE x 8'-6" LONG
(10) 90# BAGS OF READY MIX CEMENT

CLIMBING WALL

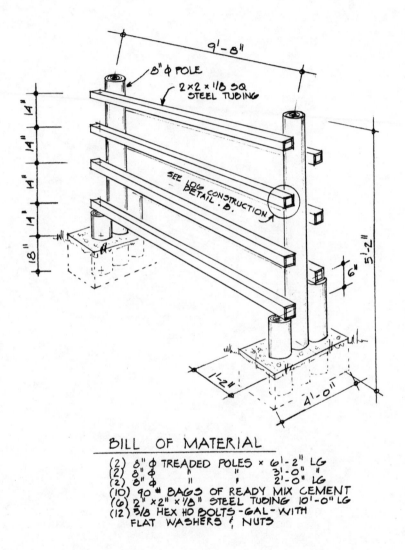

BILL OF MATERIAL

(2) 8" φ TREADED POLES × 6'-2" LG
(2) 8" φ   "   "   3'-0" "
(2) 8" φ   "   "   2'-0" LG
(10) 90# BAGS OF READY MIX CEMENT
(6) 2" × 2" × 1/8" STEEL TUBING 10'-0" LG
(12) 5/8 HEX HD BOLTS - GAL - WITH
     FLAT WASHERS & NUTS

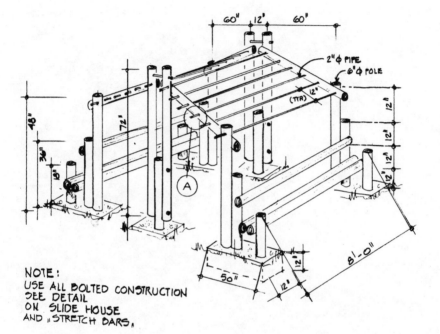

NOTE:
USE ALL BOLTED CONSTRUCTION
SEE DETAIL
ON SLIDE HOUSE
AND "STRETCH BARS.

BILL OF MATERIAL

(16) 90# BAGS OF CEMENT
(4) 6" Φ TREATED WOOD POLE × 50"
(4) 6" Φ   "   "   × 18"
(4) 6" Φ   "   "   × 60'
(4) 6" Φ   "   "   × 84"
(4) 6" Φ   "   "   × 72'
(6) 6" Φ   "   "   × 84"
(10) 2" GAL SCH 40 PIPE × 84"
(20) 3/8 × 5" GAL LAG BOLTS
(4) 3/4" TREATED ROD × 36" LG
(8) 3/4"   "   "   × 20" LG

BALANCE BRIDGE

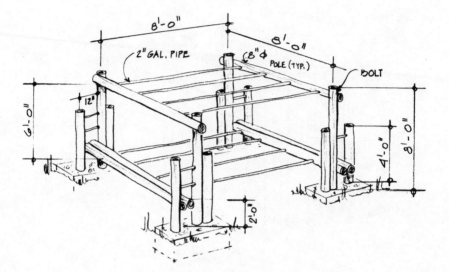

BILL OF MATERIAL

(12) 90# BAGS OF CEMENT
(4) 8" φ TREATED WOOD POLE × 8'-0"
(8) 8" φ   "   "   " × 5'-0"
(6) 8" φ   "   "   " × 9'-0"
(8) 2" GAL PIPE SCH 40 × 8'-0"
(6) 2"   "   " SCH 40 × 1'-6"

USE ALL BOLTED CONSTRUCTION

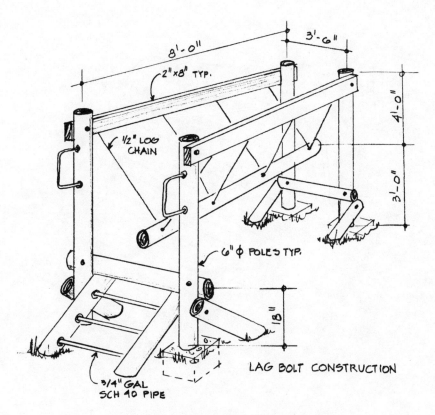

8'-0"

2"x8" TYP.

3'-6"

4'-0"

½" LOG CHAIN

3'-0"

6" φ POLES TYP.

18"

LAG BOLT CONSTRUCTION

¾" GAL SCH 40 PIPE

BILL OF MATERIAL

(4) 6" φ TREATED WOOD POLE x 8'-0"
(1) 6" φ   "   "   " x 7'-0"
(2) 2"x8"   "   "   " x 8'-0"
(2) 6" φ   "   "   POLE x 3'-6"
(6) 6" φ   "   "   " x 3'-0"
(3) ¾" GAL SCH 40 PIPE x 3'-0"
(36) 5/8 LAG BOLTS 7" LG
(24) ½" GAL LOGGING CHAIN

SADDLE

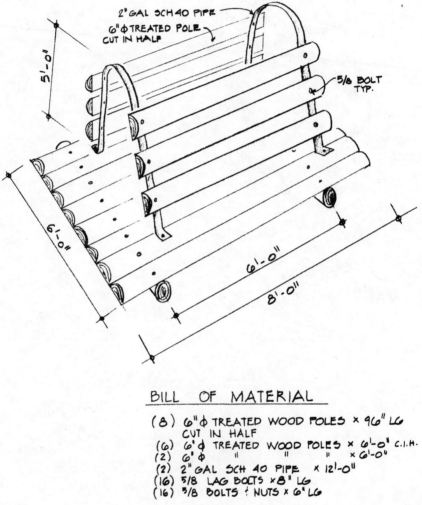

2" GAL SCH 40 PIPE
6" Ø TREATED POLE
CUT IN HALF

5'-0"

5/8 BOLT
TYP.

6'-0"

6'-0"

8'-0"

BILL OF MATERIAL

(8) 6" Ø TREATED WOOD POLES × 96" LG
  CUT IN HALF
(6) 6' Ø TREATED WOOD POLES × 6'-0" C.I.H.
(2) 6" Ø   "   "   "   × 6'-0"
(2) 2" GAL SCH 40 PIPE × 12'-0"
(16) 5/8 LAG BOLTS × 8" LG
(16) 5/8 BOLTS & NUTS × 6" LG

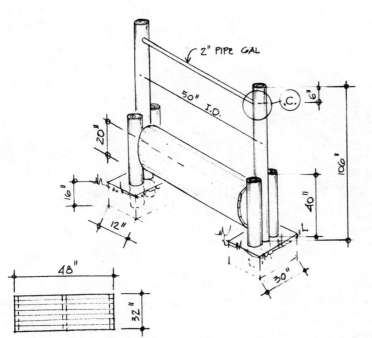

2" PIPE GAL

50" I.D.

20"

6"

12"

48"

32"

106"

40"

6"

30"

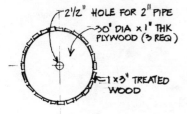

2½" HOLE FOR 2" PIPE

30" DIA × 1" THK PLYWOOD (3 REQ)

1×3" TREATED WOOD

BILL OF MATERIAL

DRUM
(3) PCS 1" PLYWOOD (TREATED) CUT INTO 30" DIA CIRCLE
(31) PCS 1"×3" TREATED WOOD × 48" LG
OTHER
(6) 90# BAGS OF CEMENT
(2) 2" SCH 40 GAL STEEL PIPE × 58½"
(4) ½" LAG BOLTS × 7" LG
(2) 8" ⌀ TREATED WOOD POLES × 118"
(4) 8" ⌀ " " " × 52" LG

119

LOG CABIN I

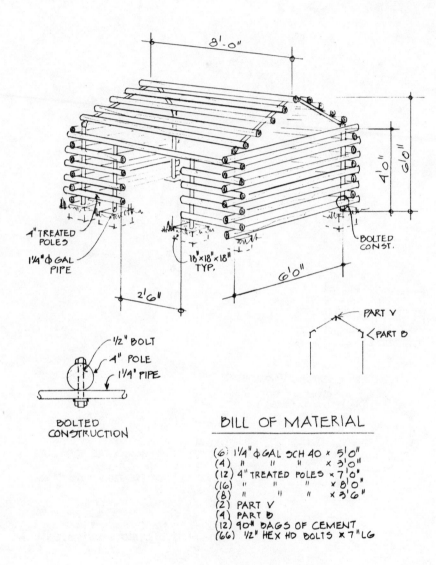

8'-0"

6'-0"

4'-0"

4" TREATED
POLES

1¼"⌀ GAL
PIPE

2'-6"

18"×18"×18"
TYP.

6'-0"

BOLTED
CONST.

PART V

PART D

½" BOLT

4" POLE

1¼" PIPE

**BOLTED
CONSTRUCTION**

BILL OF MATERIAL

(6) 1¼"⌀ GAL SCH 40 × 5'0"
(4) " " " × 3'0"
(12) 4" TREATED POLES × 7'0"
(16) " " " × 8'0"
(8) " " " × 3'6"
(2) PART V
(4) PART D
(12) 90# BAGS OF CEMENT
(66) ½" HEX HD BOLTS × 7"LG

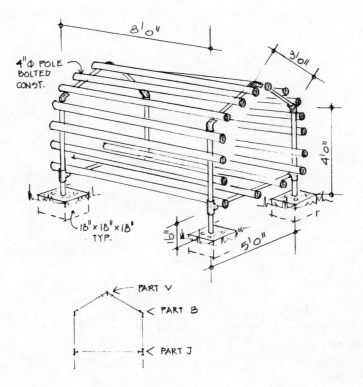

4" Ø POLE
BOLTED
CONST.

8'0"

3'0"

4'0"

18" × 18" × 18"
TYP.

5'0"

PART V

PART B

PART J

BILL OF MATERIAL

(4) 1¼" GAL PIPE × 6'0"
(4) "   "   " × 3'0"
(2) "   "   " × 5'0"
(16) 4" TREATED WOOD POLES × 10'0"
(2) PART V
(4) PART B
(4) PART J
(32) ½" HEX HD BOLTS × 7" LG
(8) 90# BAGS OF CEMENT

STRETCH BARS

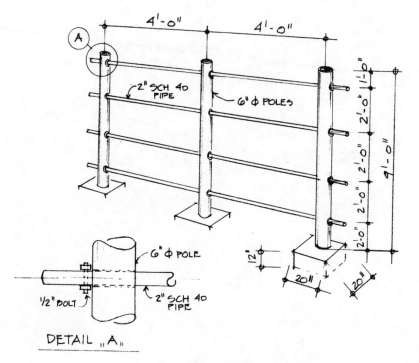

4'-0"   4'-0"

A

2" SCH 40 PIPE

6" ⌀ POLES

1'-0"
2'-0"
2'-0"
2'-0"
9'-0"

12"
20"
20"

6" ⌀ POLE

1/2" BOLT

2" SCH 40 PIPE

DETAIL "A"

BILL OF MATERIAL

(3) 6" ⌀ TREATED WOOD POLES x 10'-0"
(4) 2" SCH 40 PLATED PIPE x 10'-0"
(6) 90# BAGS OF READY MIX CEMENT
(8) 1/2" PLATED BOLTS x 3" W/ LOCK NUTS

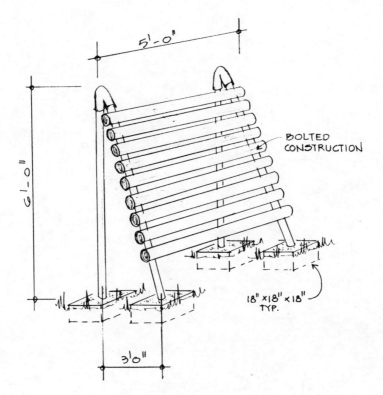

5'-0"

6'-0"

BOLTED CONSTRUCTION

18" X 18" X 18" TYP.

3'0"

BILL OF MATERIAL

(8) 90# BAGS OF CEMENT
(4) 1¼" GAL POLES SCH 40 × 8'0"
(2) PART I
(9) 4" Ø POLES × 5'0"
20 ½" HEX HD BOLTS × 7" LG

123

FITNESS LADDER

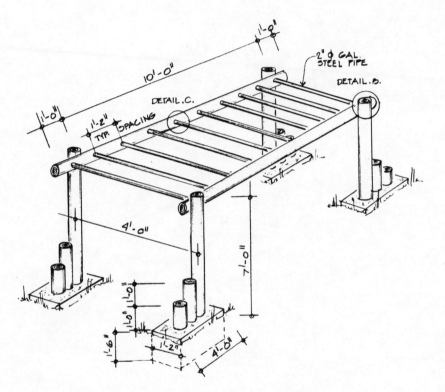

Detail dimensions and labels: 1'-0", 10'-0", 2" ⌀ GAL. STEEL PIPE, DETAIL .B., DETAIL .C., 1'-0", 1'-2" TYP. SPACING, 4'-0", 7'-0", 1'-0", 1'-0", 1'-6", 1'-2", 4'-0"

BILL OF MATERIAL

(2) 8" ⌀ TREATED WOOD POLES x 12'-0" LG
(4) 8" ⌀   "   "   "   8'-6"   "
(4) 0" ⌀   "   "   "   3'-0" LG
(4) 8" ⌀   "   "   "   2'-0"   "
(30) 90# BAGS OF READY MIX CEMENT
(10) 2" ⌀ GAL STEEL PIPE SCH 40 x 60" LG
(4) 1" HEX HD BOLT & NUT - GAL. x 16" LG

CLIMBING POLE

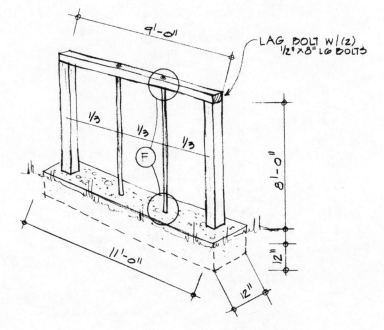

9'-0"

LAG BOLT W/ (2)
1/2" X 8" LG BOLTS

1/3   1/3   1/3

F

8'-0"

11'-0"

12"

12"

BILL OF MATERIAL

(3) PCS 4" x 4" TREATED WOOD 9'-0" LG
(2) PCS 1 1/2" SCH 40 PIPE x 9'-0" LG
(10) 90# BAGS OF CEMENT
(4) 1/2" GAL LAG BOLTS x 8" LG

MONKEY SLIDING POLE

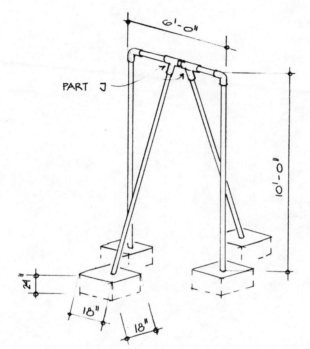

PART J

6'-0"

10'-0"

24"

18"

18"

BILL OF MATERIAL

(4) 1¼"⌀ GAL SCH 40
    PIPE × 12'-0" LG
(1) 1¼"⌀ GAL SCH 40
    PIPE × 6'-0" LG
(2) 90° ELL PART D
(2) TEES PART J
(8) 90# BAGS OF CEMENT

126

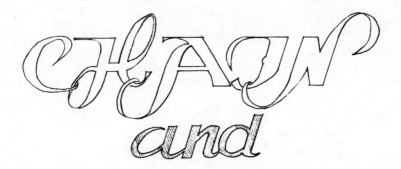

MONKEY CRAWL

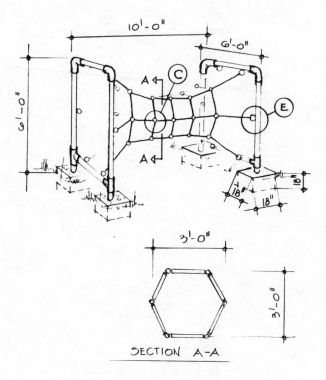

SECTION A-A

BILL OF MATERIAL

(8) 90# BAGS OF CEMENT
(8) 1¼"Ø GAL PIPE x 6'-0" LG
(4) 90° ELL PART D
(2) TEES PART J
80' ½" LOGGING CHAIN
22 PC RUBBER HOSE (CUT TO SIZE)
12 ½" EYE BOLTS x 4" LG

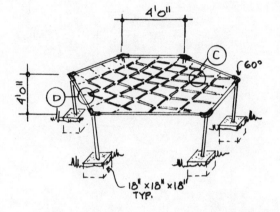

4'0"

4'0"

C

60°

D

18" × 18" × 18"
TYP.

BILL OF MATERIAL

(6) 60° ELLS PART G
(12) 90# BAGS OF CEMENT
(6) 1¼" ∅ PIPE × 4'0"
(6) "   " × 6'0"
120' ½" LOGGING CHAIN
    RUBBER HOSE CUT TO LENGTH
(24) ½" EYE BOLTS × 4" LG

129

MONKEY CLIMB

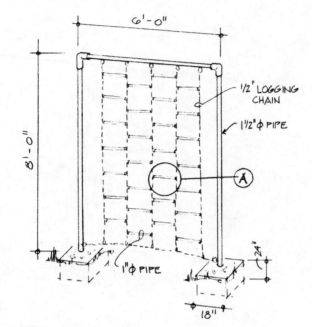

6'-0"

8'-0"

1/2" LOGGING CHAIN

1 1/2" ⌀ PIPE

Ⓐ

24"

18"

1" ⌀ PIPE

BILL OF MATERIAL

(2) CLAMPS PART D
(1) 1 1/4" ⌀ PIPE × 6'-0"
(2) 1 1/4" ⌀ PIPE × 10'-0"
(6) 90# BAGS OF CEMENT
(28) 1" ⌀ SCH 40 PIPE × 12" LG
(70') 1/2" PLATED LOGGING CHAIN
(5) 1/2" EYE BOLTS × 4" LG
     PC RUBBER HOSE (CUT TO SIZE)

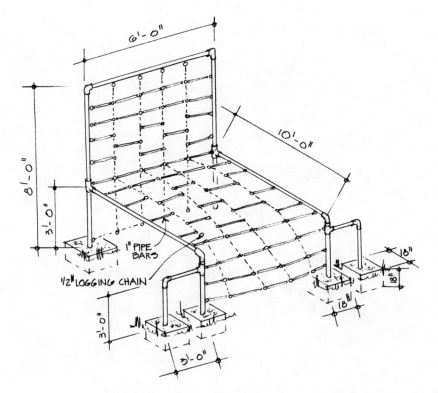

6'-0"

8'-0"

3'-0"

10'-0"

1" PIPE BARS

1/2" LOGGING CHAIN

3'-0"

3'-0"

18"

18"

18"

BILL OF MATERIAL

(6) 90° ELL   PART D
(4) TEES   PART J
(2) 1 1/4" Ø PIPE GAL SCH 40 × 10'0" LG
(1)   "   "   "   "   "   × 6'0"   "
(6)   "   "   "   "   "   × 3'-0" "
(4)   "   "   "   "   "   × 5'0"   "
110' 1/2" LOGGING CHAIN
60 PC 1" PIPE SCH 40 GAL × 12"
35 1/2" EYE BOLTS × 4" LG

131

MONKEY UNITS
DETAILS

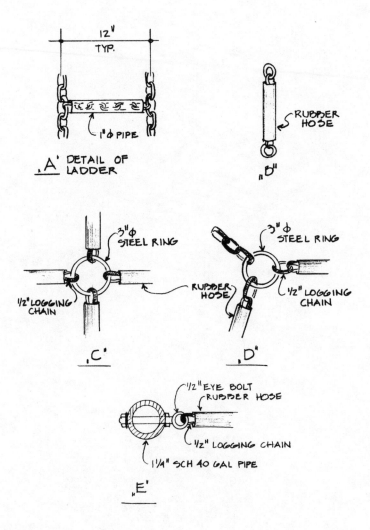

12" TYP.

1"Ø PIPE

"A" DETAIL OF LADDER

RUBBER HOSE

"B"

3"Ø STEEL RING

1/2" LOGGING CHAIN

"C"

3"Ø STEEL RING

RUBBER HOSE

1/2" LOGGING CHAIN

"D"

1/2" EYE BOLT
RUBBER HOSE

1/2" LOGGING CHAIN

1 1/4" SCH 40 GAL PIPE

"E"

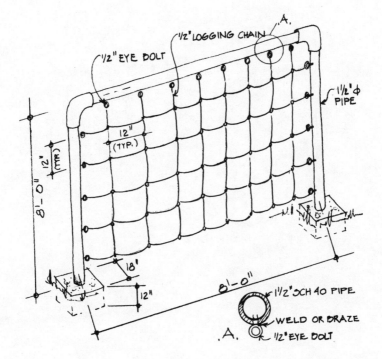

1/2" LOGGING CHAIN

1/2" EYE BOLT

A.

1 1/2" φ PIPE

12" (TYP.)

8'-0"

12" (MIN)

18"

12"

8'-0"

1 1/2" SCH 40 PIPE

WELD OR BRAZE

1/2" EYE BOLT

A.

BILL OF MATERIAL

(4) 90# BAGS OF CEMENT
(2) 90° SCREWED GAL ELLBOW TREATED, SCH 40
(3) 1 1/2" NPS GAL SCH 40 PIPE × 8'-6" LG
110' 1/2" PLATED LOGGING CHAIN
21 1/2" EYE BOLTS × 2" LG

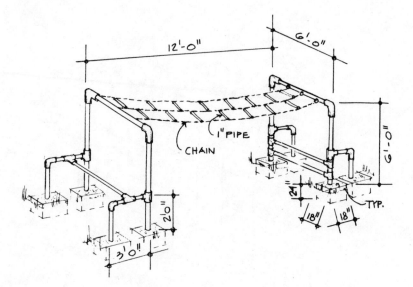

12'-0" 6'-0"

1" PIPE

CHAIN

6'-0"

2'-0"

2'0"

3'-0"

18" 18"

TYP.

BILL OF MATERIAL

(9) 1¼"⌀ GAL SCH 40 PIPE x 6'0"
(4) "   "   "   "   "   x 3'0"
(4) "   "   "   "   "   x 2'0"
(8) 90° ELLS PART D
(10) TEES PART J
(16) 90# BAGS OF CEMENT
60' ½" LOGGING CHAIN
16 1" SCH 40 GAL PIPE x 18" LG
(6) ½" EYE BOLTS x 4" LG

134

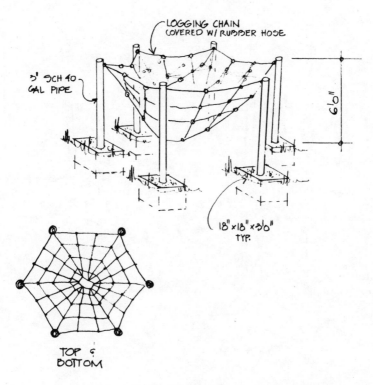

LOGGING CHAIN
COVERED W/ RUBBER HOSE

5' SCH 40
GAL PIPE

6'-0"

18"×18"×3'-0"
TYP.

TOP &
BOTTOM

BILL OF MATERIAL

(12) 90# BAGS OF CEMENT
(6) 5/8 EYE BOLTS × 5" LG
200' 1/2" LOGGING CHAIN
RUBBER HOSE CUT TO LENGTH

135

SPIDER WEB II

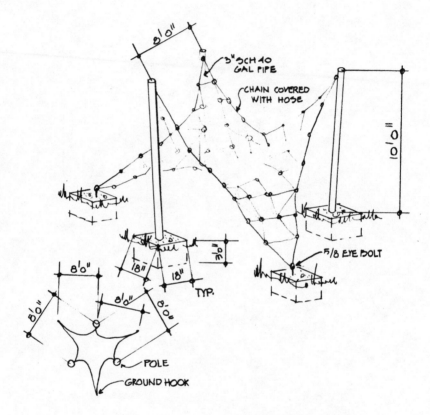

8'0"

3" SCH 40
GAL PIPE

CHAIN COVERED
WITH HOSE

10'0"

5/8 EYE BOLT

12'0"

18" 18"

TYP.

8'0"

8'0" 8'0"

8'0"

POLE

GROUND HOOK

BILL OF MATERIAL

(3) 3" SCH 40 GAL PIPE × 12'0"
(3) 5/8" × 18" EYE BOLTS
(3) 5/8" × 6"   "   "
260' 1/2" LOGGING CHAIN
    RUBBER HOSE CUT TO LENGTH

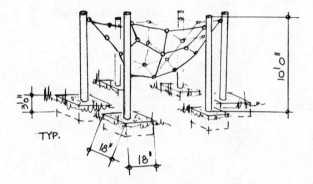

TYP.

30"

18" 18"

10'-0"

BILL OF MATERIAL

(12) 90# BAGS OF CEMENT
(6) 3" ⌀ GAL PIPE SCH 40 × 12'-0"
(6) 5/8 EYE BOLTS × 6"
200' 1/2" LOGGING CHAIN
       RUBBER HOSE CUT TO LENGTH

STANDARD PIPE CLAMPS

FOR 1½" ⌀ GAL SCH 40 PIPE

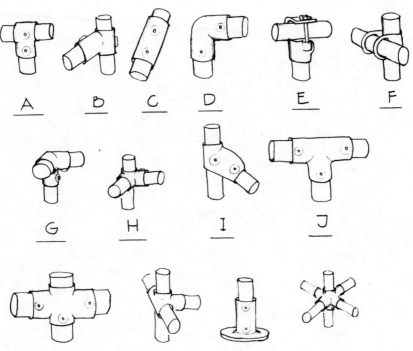

A   B   C   D   E   F

G   H   I   J

K   L   M   N

PAGE 1

138

STANDARD PIPE CLAMPS
FOR 1½" Ø GAL SCH 40 PIPE

O

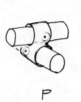

P

Q

R

S

T

U

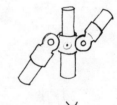

V

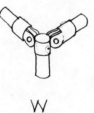

W

X

Y

Z

PAGE 2

139

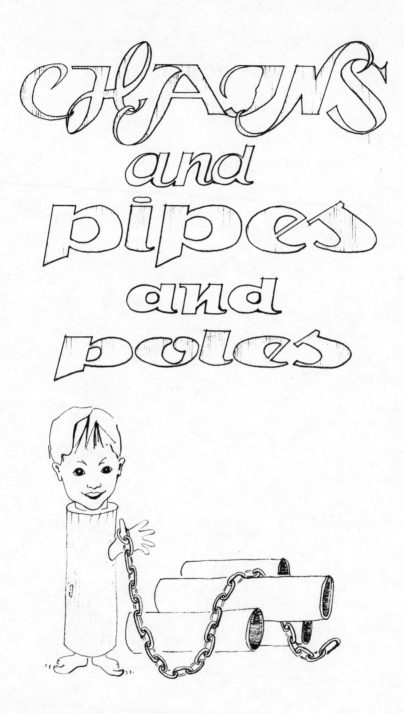

CHAINS
and
pipes
and
poles

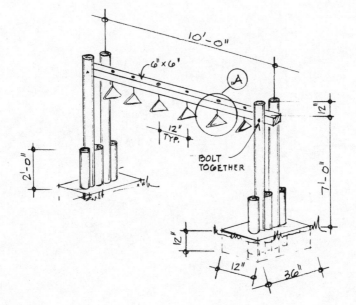

BILL OF MATERIAL

(1) 6" × 6" TREATED WOOD × 11'-0"
(4) 6" φ   "   POLES × 9'-0"
(6) 6" φ   "   "   × 3'-0"
(6) 90# BAGS OF READY MIX CEMENT
(2) 3/4" PLATED BOLTS × 20" LG
    COMPLETE W/WASHERS & NUTS
(6) HAND HOLDS - SEE DETAIL "A"

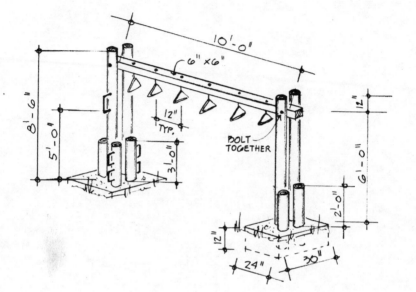

BILL OF MATERIAL

(1) 6" x 6" TREATED WOOD x 11'-0"
(2) 6" ∅ " POLES x 8'-0"
(2) 6" ∅ " " x 10'-6"
(4) 6" ∅ " " x 3'-0"
(2) 6" ∅ " " x 4'-0"
(6) 90# BAGS OF READY MIX CEMENT
(2) 3/4" PLATED BOLTS x 20" LG, COMPLETE
    WITH FLAT WASHERS & NUTS
(6) HAND HOLDS SEE DETAIL "A"

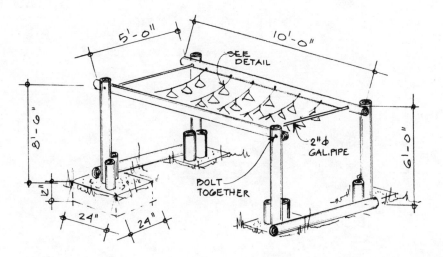

BILL OF MATERIAL

(2) 6" φ TREATED POLES × 11'-0"
(2) 6" φ   "   "   × 8'-0"
(2) 6" φ   "   "   × 10'-6"
(4) 6" φ   "   "   × 3'-0"
(4) 6" φ   "   "   × 4'-0"
(2) 6" φ   "   "   × 7'-0"
(6) 90# BAGS OF READY MIX CEMENT
(2) 2" GAL SCH 40 PIPE × 5'-0" LG
(4) ¾" PLATED BOLTS × 20" LG, COMPLETE
    WITH FLAT WASHERS & NUTS
(24) HAND HOLDS (SEE DETAIL "B")
80' ¾" LOGGING CHAIN (PLATED)
(12) ½" PLATED HEX BOLT × 1½" LG
    WITH FLAT WASHERS & LOCK NUTS

143

DETAILS OF
HAND HOLDS

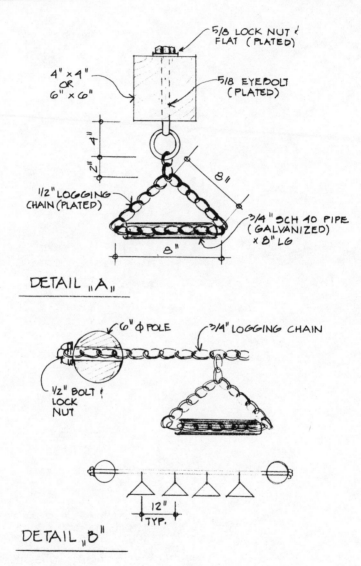

5/8 LOCK NUT &
FLAT (PLATED)

4" x 4"
OR
6" x 6"

5/8 EYEBOLT
(PLATED)

4"

2"

1/2" LOGGING
CHAIN (PLATED)

8"

3/4" SCH 40 PIPE
(GALVANIZED)
x 8" LG

8"

DETAIL "A"

6" ∅ POLE

3/4" LOGGING CHAIN

1/2" BOLT &
LOCK
NUT

12"
TYP.

DETAIL "B"

CHAIN LADDER CLIMBER

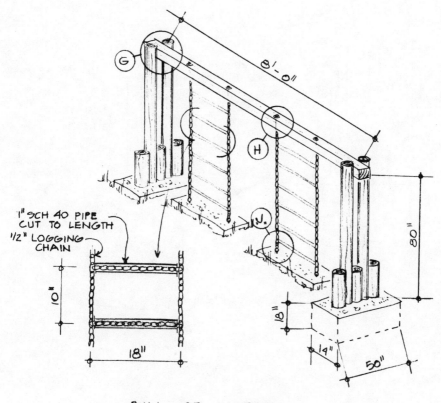

1" SCH 40 PIPE
CUT TO LENGTH

1/2" LOGGING
CHAIN

8'-0"

80"

18"

14"

50"

10"

18"

BILL OF MATERIAL

(4) 6"ϕ TREATED WOOD POLE × 102" LG
(6) 6"ϕ   "   "   "   × 34" LG
(15) 90# BAGS OF CEMENT
(2) 1"ϕ GAL BOLT × 20" LG
(4) 1/2" GAL LOGGING CHAIN × 80" LG
(14) 1/2"   "   "   "   × 18" LG
(14) 1" SCH GAL 40 PIPE × 18" LG
(8) 1/2" EYE BOLTS × 7" LG

CHAIN BALANCE

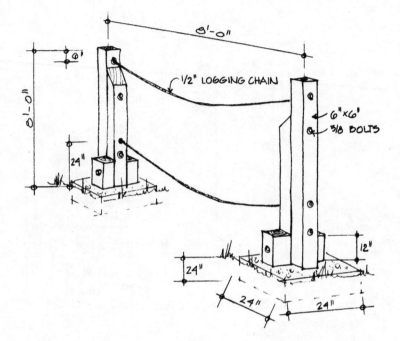

8'-0"

½" LOGGING CHAIN

6"x6"

3/8 BOLTS

8'-0"

6"

24"

24"

12"

24"

24"

BILL OF MATERIAL

22' OF ½" PLATED LOGGING CHAIN
(2) 6" x 6" TREATED WOOD POLES x 10'-0"
(2) 6" x 6"   "   "   "   x 7'-0"
(4) 6" x 6"   "   "   "   x 3'-0"
(16) 90# BAGS OF CEMENT

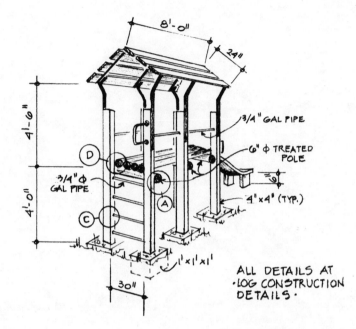

8'-0"

24"

3/4" GAL PIPE

6" ⌀ TREATED POLE

D

4'-6"

3/4" ⌀ GAL PIPE

A

4'-0"

C

4"x4" (TYP.)

1'x1'x1'

30"

**ALL DETAILS AT
·LOG CONSTRUCTION
DETAILS·**

BILL OF MATERIAL

(6) 1"x 8" SHEETING x 8'-0"
(6) 4"x4" TREATED WOOD x 8'-0"
(3) 6" ⌀   "   "   x 3B"
(1) 6' ⌀   "   "   x 8'-0"
(2) 3/4" GAL PIPE x 8'-0"
(4) 3/4'   "   "   x 36"
(10) 90# BAGS OF CEMENT
(1) S.S. SLIDE
(6) 3/4"x12" GAL BOLTS & NUTS
(12) 3/4"x14"   "   "   "
(8) 3/8 x5" GAL HEX HD BOLTS